I0710154

Reaching America's Potential

Volume 1
Healthcare
Shared Economics
Taxes

Thomas A. Rabatin

Amazon Kindle

Healthcare, Shared Economics, and Taxes

Copyright

Dedicated to *America* and *Voters Like You*

This book is dedicated to America and Voters Like You who are disappointed, frustrated, and angry that America has not reach its true potential, who understand that Reaching America's Potential is needed, possible, and viable, and who believe America should never stop the quest, journey, and mission of Reaching America's Potential. Comparing America to other countries is a waste of time, not productive, and counterproductive. One can always find countries that are not as great, good, or powerful as America. This leads America to become complacent, self-satisfied, and unmoved to improve. Present America should be measured, gaged, and compared to Past America to determine America's current direction, path, and trajectory for Future America. This assessment determines whether America is declining, standing still, or improving.

The reality is no matter how great America is it can always improve becoming better, richer, and greater.

Sincerely,

Thomas A. Rabatin

Table of Contents

Preface

Election cycle after election cycle, presidential campaign slogans inundated, overwhelmed, and mesmerized voters:

- via the airways,
- on campaign fliers,
- on yard signs,
- on billboards,
- via radio, TV, and internet political commercials,
- at political rallies,
- thru political stump speeches,
- in newspaper ads, and
- on political talk shows.

For each presidential election cycle, there is renewed expectation, revived inspiration, and restored conviction that this time, the campaign slogans would be realized, achieved, and attained. For each presidential election cycle, these political slogans, mantras, themes, and talking points turn out to be meaningless, useless, and worthless lacking transformations, renovations, and modifications. Each time, disappointment is replaced by hope that the next presidential cycle would be different where slogans would *"Walk the Talk."*

The following are presidential campaign slogans from 1968 thru 2016[1]:

- In 1968, Nixon's slogan, "This time, vote like your whole world depended on it", resulted in 7 more years of the Vietnam War, and the additional deaths of 37,794 U.S. soldiers.[2]
- In 1972, Nixon's slogan, "Nixon Now", was replaced by Watergate, resignation, and disgrace.
- In 1976, Carter's slogan, "Not Just Peanuts", was followed by the failed rescue of 50 U.S embassy hostages and the highest 4-year inflation total of 41.5%.[3]
- In 1980, Reagan's slogan, "Are You Better Off Than You Were Four Years Ago?", began the war against workers' unions, dismantled the air traffic controllers' union, stained by the suicide bombing of 243 marines, and concluded with the invasion of Grenada, a small island.[4]
- In 1984, Reagan's slogan, "It's Morning Again in America", initiated the illegal sale of arms to Iran and the sale of illegal drugs in the U.S. to fund Reagan's unlawful Contra war against the Nicaraguan Sandinista government.[5]
- In 1988, Bush senior's slogan, "Kinder, Gentler Nation", pardon all those associated with the Iran-Contra[6] criminal syndicate, invaded Kuwait and Iraq, vetoed the Civil Rights Act, and sent U.S. troops to Somalia[7].

- In 1992, Clinton's slogan "It's the economy, stupid" resulted in the passage of NAFTA, the loss of 150,000 U.S. jobs, and the suppression U.S. wages[8]. Which economy was the slogan referring to the U.S. economy or the Mexican economy?
- In 1996, Clinton's "Building a bridge to the twenty-first century" did not result in infrastructure investments[9].
- In 2000, Bush junior's "Compassionate Conservatism" misled the U.S. about weapons of mass destruction, attacked Iraq, rejected the Kyoto Protocol to reduce CO^2, passed the Bush's tax cuts which mostly benefited the upper and upper-middle class, and authorize enhance interrogation, the torture of prisoners of war, wartime crime[10].
- In 2004, Bush junior's "A Safer World and a More Hopeful America" passes tax benefits for oil and gas industry, bungled the federal response to Hurricane Katrina, banned same-sex marriage, and vetoed stem cell research[11].
- In 2008, Obama's "Hope and Change" conjured up a lot of hope with few changes.
- In 2012, Obama's "Forward" was never realized as the status quo remained.
- In 2016, Trump's "Make America Great Again" was never met, as Trump insulted the world, as millions protested the Trump administration, as he withdrew from the Trans-Pacific Partnership, as he reversed environmental pollution protections, as he

legitimizes the white nationalists and neo-Nazis, as he started a losing trade war with China, as he withdrew from Iran Nuclear Deal, as he bungled the pandemic response resulting in the unnecessary death of 100's of thousands, as he unnecessarily shut down the government, as he orchestrated the siege of congress and as congress impeach him twice[12].

Clearly, Democratic and Republican presidents have sold false hopes, false futures, and false outcomes to the America public to get elected but have failed to deliver on their slogans' promises.

The genesis of the series, *Reaching America's Potential,* began years ago as a seed of discontentment, disappointment, and disillusionment with U.S. presidents and U.S. politics. Election cycle's hopes, inspirations, and visions faded into the sunset disappearing into the night. As election cycles passed, the seed sprouted into a seedling of disillusionments, grew into a small tree of disappointments, and, finally, matured into a fruit tree of crucial, essential, and vital solutions. Detours, dead ends, interruptions, and obstacles delayed the creation of *Reaching America's Potential*.

Sincerely,

Thomas A. Rabatin

Introduction

The series, *Reaching America's Potential*, will inspire a president and the voting public to realize the true potential of the U.S. *Reaching America's Potential*. The series include topics that will increase America's wealth for businesses, and the upper, upper-middle, working, and lower classes. Issues, problems, and opportunities have been thoroughly described, researched, and analyzed. The methods, strategies, and tactics for their implementation are the recipes, the plans, and the instructions for insuring the realization of America's true, full, and real potential.

Volume 1 includes the following topics:

- Healthcare,
- Shared Economics, and
- Taxes.

Chapter 1: Reduce Healthcare Cost by 70% may seem improbable, unlikely, and even impossible. However, the combined healthcare savings of:

- Medicare Free Choice Act,
- Federal Health Maintenance Organization Act,
- Global Purchasing Prescription Drugs Act,
- Preventive Healthcare Act, and
- Reducing Unnecessary Healthcare Act

is 70%.

The U.S. ranks near the bottom of developed countries in healthcare statistics while having the most expensive healthcare in the world. Because of these two startling, alarming and surprising facts, it is highly likely, not much of a leap, and totally accomplishable to reduce healthcare cost by 70% and to improve U.S. Healthcare statistics. This chapter not only outlines the current problems with U.S. Healthcare but also outlines the solutions and more importantly the methods for implementing these solutions.

Voters Like You will need to elect a president and politicians that support the above healthcare acts.

Chapter 2: Shared Economics Increases Pay and Profits may seem implausible, counterintuitive, and illogical. Shared Economics is the sharing of the profits with the employees and businesses. Shared Economics has a historical precedence and has worked in the past. This chapter compares, contrasts, and relates Shared Economics with Supply Side Economics and Demand Side Economics. This chapter outlines why Shared Economics increases pay and profits.

Voters Like You will need to elect a president and politicians that support Shared Economics.

Chapter 3: Taxing Fair and Balance replaces income tax with 1.5% sales, a 1.5% property tax, and a 10% Defense Import tax. These taxes fully fund the U.S. government and overtime pays off the national debt.

Currently, income taxes reduce the U.S. GDP growth, the income, and the wealth for businesses and the upper, upper-middle, middle, working, and lower classes. *Taxing Fair and Balance* is accomplished by having the same tax rate for everyone and all organizations. The current income tax rules, regulations and laws favor, benefit, and reduce taxes for businesses, the upper class, and the upper-middle class at the expense of over-taxing the middle class, the working class, and lower class.

Voters Like You will need to elect a president and politicians that support *Taxing Fair and Balance*.

Sincerely,

Thomas A. Rabatin

Prologue

If you are reading this book, you are frustrated, angry, and disappointed with America, America politicians and America presidents. *Reaching America's Potential* is the pathway, the trajectory, and the course that America could, should, and needs travel.

If America is not improving, then it is either static, stationary, and standing still or it is declining, weakening, and deteriorating.

You have many unanswered questions pertaining to Reaching *America's Potential in Healthcare, Shared Economics and Taxes*:

- Is it even possible?
- What are the opportunities for America?
- What are America's unrealized possibilities?
- Why hasn't it happened?
- What are the goals?
- What are the plans?
- Who can make this a reality?
- With so little free time, can I really help?
- How can I help?

These questions and many more are researched, explored, and answered in the series *Reaching America's Potential Volume 1: Healthcare, Shared Economics and Taxes.*

Thomas A. Rabatin

Chapter 1: Reduce Healthcare Cost by 70%

The combined healthcare savings of:

- ***Medicare Free Choice Act (MFCA)*** results in savings of 21% to 31% where those under the age of 65 have the option to buy either Medicare insurance or private for-profit healthcare insurance,
- ***Federal Health Maintenance Organization Act (FHMOA)*** results in savings 40% to 50% where anyone can choice to join,
- ***Global Purchasing Prescription Drugs Act (GPPDA)*** results in savings of 40% to 60% where anyone has the choice to buy prescription drugs from other countries or from U.S.,
- ***Preventive Healthcare Act (PHA)*** results in savings of 40% to 75% where preventive healthcare proactively reduces and eliminates illnesses, and identifies illnesses in their beginning stages when mitigation and treatment are more effective and at a lower cost, and
- ***Reducing Unnecessary Healthcare Act (RUHA)*** results in a savings of 20% where unnecessary healthcare procedures, surgeries,

and treatments are identified, published, and available throughout the healthcare industry.

The combined savings of these acts result in a 70% reduction in healthcare costs while improving the U.S. healthcare statistics.

Medicare Free Choice Act (MFCA)

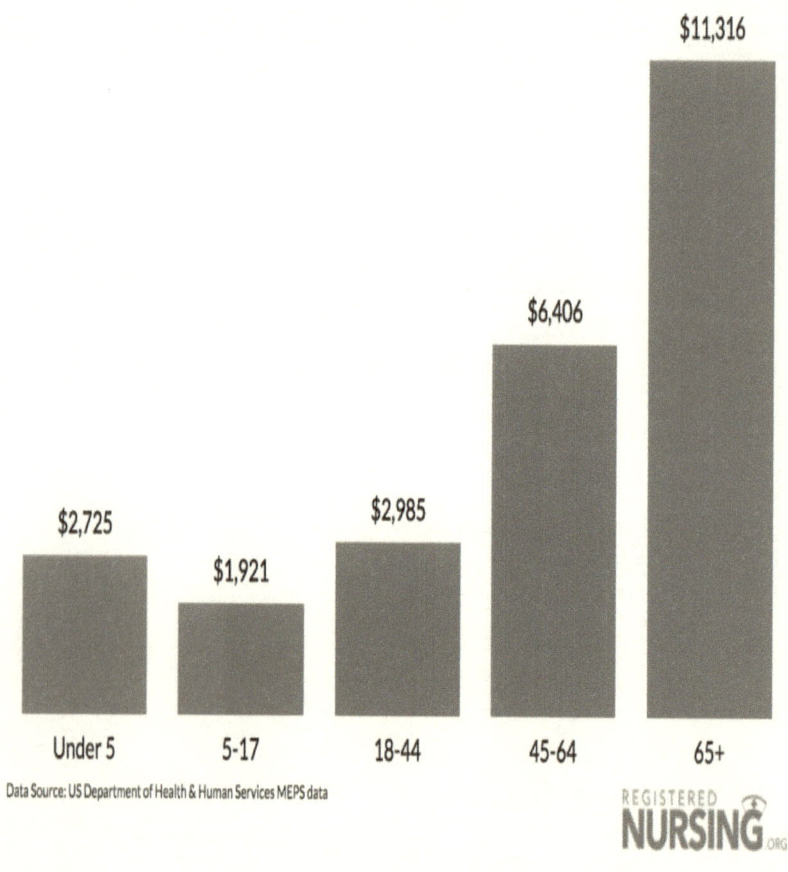

Medicare is run by the federal government and is the primary healthcare insurance for those age 65 and older. Prior to 1965, over 56% of seniors lacked medical insurance. Many privately-owned healthcare insurance companies for their profit reasons and because of the high healthcare cost for those 65 and older, either refused to cover seniors or made healthcare insurance premiums so expensive that seniors could not pay for this privately owned, for-profit healthcare insurance. In 1965, a democratically controlled congress passed the Medicare Bill which President Johnson signed into law. For one to understand the value and importance of Medicare, one should discuss it with their grandparents or anyone who is 65 and older and has Medicare. Despite being a government run program, Medicare is the largest healthcare insurance provider and is very popular with a 75% approval rating in favor of Medicare for not just themselves but also for their family members.

Medicare administrative cost is just 2% whereas private insurance administrative cost is between 12% and 18%. Therefore, privately-owned healthcare insurance cost is between 10% and 16% more expensive than Medicare according to Bernie Sanders.[13] Private health insurance companies are only required to pay 80% to 85% of patient premiums for actual patient healthcare costs according to Verywell Health.[14]

Combining the additional healthcare administrative costs with the allowable revenue margins implies that private insurance companies' costs are between 13% and 18% higher than Medicare for the same level of healthcare.

This does not include the additional costs required by medical healthcare providers to comply with the different healthcare insurance methods, forms, requirements, rules, and procedures for submitting, recording, and being reimbursed from the 900 different privately-owned healthcare insurance companies. About ½ of these medical providers' administrative costs are for billing and insurance-related expenses. This results in between 8.4% and 13.9% additional cost above the actual healthcare cost according to Healthcare Media.[15] Therefore, private insurance companies' costs are between 21.4% and 31.9% more expensive than Medicare for the same level of healthcare.

Rather than replace the privately-owned insurance companies with a single government mandated insurance provider, Medicare, those under the age of 65 could choose to buy Medicare or privately-owned healthcare insurance. This free-market choice will permit the public and businesses, *not the government,* to choose between privately-owned medical insurance or Medicare. Medicare insurance will reduce healthcare insurance costs between 21% and 31%.

Misleading Arguments against MFCA:

The government has unfair advantages over privately-owned companies who will have a difficult time competing against Medicare.

Really! What are the advantages that the government possesses over privately-owned companies? Is it that the government has no obligation to make profits for executives, shareholders, and investors who then become wealthy? The privately-owned insurance companies are required to make additional income above the patients' healthcare costs and to give that additional income to the executives, shareholders, and investors. 21% to 31% additional healthcare overheads in costs, expenses, and profits are not related nor contribute to patient healthcare, thus, unnecessarily creating more expensive healthcare for patients.

Medicare Free Choice eliminates many privately-owned healthcare insurance jobs.

This argument implies, predicts, and forecasts that the public is choosing Medicare over the privately-owned healthcare insurance. In that case, Medicare would need more employees, a larger staff, and more administrators. Many of these new Medicare employees would be recruited from the privately-owned healthcare insurance companies. Their experiences, skills, and positions that were previously employed in the private sector are now required to meet the increased, additional, and surging demand for Medicare. Medicare Free Choice would employ former employees of privately-owned insurance companies for positions such as enrollees, verifiers, specialists, customer care workers, supervisors, and managers. The reality is that Medicare would hire 90% of privately-owned healthcare insurance employees. Some of the high-level executives, managers, and supervisors would not find jobs with Medicare.

Federal Health Maintenance Organization Act

Federal Health Maintenance Organizations, Federal HMOs, would be created based on the Veterans Administration healthcare model. The Veterans Administration (VA) provides healthcare for military veterans who have served and sacrificed to protect the citizens of the United States.

The VA is the largest, the best, and the most comprehensive healthcare organization in the world. The VA has 150 hospitals, 820 Outpatient Clinics, and 300 VA Vet Centers providing healthcare to 8.92 million veterans. The VA healthcare cost is $55.4 billion at just $6,210 per VA patient. That cost per patient is incredibly low since VA patients are typically older, more likely to be disabled, and have more chronic medical conditions than the population at large. For reference, in 2014, the average Medicare cost per patients of similar demographics was just over $19,000 according to the Centers for Medicare & Medicaid Services.[16]

Non-veterans buy privately-owned healthcare on average for $321 per month or $3,852 per year. The average additional out-of-pocket healthcare expenses paid by the insured is $4,358 per year. These out-of-pocket healthcare expenses include deductibles, copays, partial cost of prescription drugs, supplemental health insurance, and coinsurances. The out-of-pocket maximum for 2020 was $8,200 for an individual and $16,400 for a family according to Policygenius.com.[17] Out-of-pocket healthcare expenses are what one needs to pay annually before the privately-owned healthcare insurance pays 100% of one's additional medical expenses. If one is healthy and not injured, then one pays $3,852 per year. However, if one becomes ill or injured, then one can expect to pay up to $12,052 per year. Incredibly, unbelievably, and sorrowfully, this is before the privately-owned healthcare insurance begins to pay 100% of one's healthcare expenses. The out-of-pocket annual deductible is the reason that many Americans delay, avoid, and postpone healthcare until illnesses become acute, problematic, and demanding or injuries become unbearable, intolerable, and unacceptable. This delay in healthcare results in more costly, expensive, and extensive medical care. However, seeking healthcare treatment sooner would act as preventative cost reduction measures resulting in less extensive healthcare and better healthcare results. The VA practices extensive, comprehensive, and exhaustive preventative healthcare and thus reduces the VA's cost of healthcare.

The VA's patients have a median age of 52 years old as compared to the U.S. median age of 37 years old. On top of that, the VA's patients suffer from higher occurrences of chronic illnesses and severe injuries resulting from their prior honorable military services.

Given these statistics, it is impressive that VA healthcare is, at a minimum, 24% lower than the cost of privately-owned healthcare according to NBC News[18].

Even with the VA spending less for healthcare than the private sector, veterans' satisfaction of their healthcare is 4% higher than non-veterans' satisfaction of their private healthcare. The National Patient Satisfaction Survey revealed that VA has a satisfaction rating of 91%, a loyalty rating of 93%, and a professionalism rating of 92%.[19] VA patients consistently rate their VA healthcare higher than non-veterans rate their privately-owned healthcare.

Misleading arguments against VA healthcare:

The VA healthcare is poorer than privately-owned healthcare.

Privately-owned healthcare companies fabricate, propagate, and spread these falsehoods, myths, and delusions to frighten the public from even considering Federal HMOs based on the VA healthcare system. Ironically, privately-owned healthcare providers make these claims while privately-owned healthcare mistakes are responsible for and directly connect to 250,000 unnecessary avoidable deaths per year according to CNBC modern medicine.[20] The U.S. privately-owned healthcare system statistically ranks near the bottom in all health wellness categories as compared to other countries as cited by the World

Health Organization. Veterans receiving medical care from the VA will attest to their outstanding healthcare.

Why does the VA provide the best healthcare in the U.S. and potentially in the world?

Providing a narrative of a veteran's healthcare experiences for comparison to non-veteran's privately-owned healthcare experiences will undoubtedly highlight the differences that make the VA healthcare system superior to privately-owned healthcare.

A veteran had 55 VA medical appointments, with each office visit scheduled and started at a specific time with only one exception. Compare this to one's typical experience of waiting hours in a doctor's waiting room. Each of the veteran's medical appointments lasted about 25 minutes. After waiting hours, the civilian's doctor spends less than 5 minutes examining one's health. One's long waits and short doctor examinations are the result of privately-owned healthcare maximizing income rather than maximizing the quality of healthcare. The VA healthcare providers are not profit driven and care about the veterans' health and have adequate time to listen to the veterans' concerns.

Hospitals are some of the most inhospitable places on this planet. Cold, sterile, and unwelcoming are just a few adjectives that come to mind when describing a place that is supposed to provide quality compassion and care. These negative adjectives, however, are all but absent for the veterans who enter the VA hospital. At many VA Medical Centers, VA volunteers offered the veterans a cup of coffee. On two occasions, the volunteers also offered donuts: one time, the veteran showing disciplined, politely stated "No thanks." On another VA visit, the veteran gave into the veteran's sugar desires and accepted the treat. On multiple occasions, Mariachi bands entertained veterans in the hospital lobby.

The veteran's surgical experience at the VA included an initial examination for determining the essential question: "Does the veteran even need surgery?" While this may seem obvious, the privately-owned healthcare, in pursuit of maximizing profits, is often all too quick to provide care when it is not necessary. The exam started on time and lasted about 30 minutes. Once determined that surgery was required, the VA Surgical team gave the veteran the choice of either a male or a female surgeon. About two weeks before surgery, the veteran had pre-operational and anesthesiology exams. Both exams started on time and lasted about 30 minutes.

How does privately-owned pre-operational healthcare compare?

The day of the veteran's surgery, the veteran reported at 10 AM to the pre-operational ward. The receptionist took the veteran into the preop staging area at 10:30 AM. The veteran remained there until 12:30 PM, about 2 hours.

During that 2 hours, a preop nurse, an anesthesiologist, a surgeon, a surgeon in training, an anesthesiologist intern and a postop nurse all utilized this window of time to explain in detail their individual responsibilities while thoroughly answering the veteran's questions and addressing the veteran's concerns.

In privately-owned surgery, do healthcare professionals answer all of one's questions?

Each VA healthcare provider verifies the veteran's birthday and the last 4 of the veteran's social security number. This is to ensure that the veteran is the correct patient. While this may seem obvious, such lapses in the privately-owned surgical space occur more frequently than one might anticipate, expect, or believe. The VA requires these safeguards to reduce if not to eliminate the cost of medical complications resulting from misidentification of the patient.

In privately-owned hospitals, the misidentification of patients results in medical errors, duplicate medical records, clinical productivity loss, and revenue loss for hospitals according to Imprivata's "The real cost of Patient Misidentification."[21] Hospitals report that 8-10% of patients are misidentified. This may be extremely low since 64% of healthcare providers responded that misidentification occur frequently or all the time.[22]

Given the hectic nature of privately-owned hospitals and the often over-capacity, under-staffed, and for-profit way that privately-owned hospitals are operated, patient handoff is one critical, important, and necessary technique required to carefully, securely, and accurately rotate patients' healthcare between physicians and nurses. Despite the importance of patient handoff, very few doctors are properly trained in the proper execution of patient handoff. This can and does lead to serious implications, complications, and injuries to patients under their care. "In a survey of 161 medical and surgical residents at the Massachusetts General Hospital conducted by Kitch and colleagues, 58% of residents reported that at least 1 patient had experienced minor harm, and 12.3% reported that at least 1 patient had experienced major harm related to handoffs."[23] The typical privately-owned healthcare includes very little of the above VA's patient identification precautions and safeguards. To privately-owned healthcare institutions, the time spent identifying, explaining, and answering patients' concerns is a gigantic, useless, and costly waste of time reducing their income and profits. Privately-owned medical blunders result in more healthcare, higher revenue, and increased income. The VA's reductions of healthcare mistakes result in less costly healthcare and in a significant savings in healthcare cost.

Prior to the veteran's surgery, the surgeon apologized to the veteran for the late start explaining that the previous surgery had taken 5 hours. The veteran was quite surprised by the surgeon's apology. Concerned, the veteran responded, "I understand that things like this happen. I hoped the operation was successful."

Do privately-owned healthcare providers apologize for patients' long waits?

The surgical nurse took the veteran back to the post-op ward. After the operation, the veteran awoke to a recovery nurse attending the veteran. The surgeon met with the veteran to discuss the surgery and the recovery from surgery. At this time, the veteran thanked the surgeon for the high quality of healthcare received at the VA and wished that the VA were a *Health Maintenance Organization that the veteran's family could join.*

HMOs are health maintenance organizations which provide medical care from doctors, hospitals, and other healthcare providers for a fixed monthly fee. Federal HMOs based on the VA medical model could provide medical care to non-veterans and should be an option for non-veterans.

In the recovery room, the surgeon, anesthesiologist, and the postop nurse, all examined and questioned the veteran to get a pulse on the veteran's current medical condition. This crucial step is taken to catch, identify and diagnose postoperative complications sooner rather than later, to improve the success of the vet's postop recovery, to enhance the vet's quality of life, and to reduce VA's healthcare expenses.

Does privately-owned surgery include these additional healthcare precautions?

For privately-owned healthcare establishments, postoperative follow up is limited or does not even exist. For medical billing, postoperative follow-up is a part of the surgical cost. Thus, privately-owned healthcare does not receive any additional funds for postoperative follow-up. Postoperative follow-up complications are viewed by privately-owned healthcare systems as additional sources of revenue and income. Their discovery is often delayed, which leads to more acute postoperative problems, and the necessity of more intensive healthcare to mitigate, address, and correct. This insures a significant increase in revenue, income, and profit for the privately-owned healthcare systems, much to the detriment of patients' health.

A few days after the veteran's operation, the surgeon, a nurse, and the primary care doctor separately called the veteran for follow-up interviews to determine the veteran's current state of health. Privately-owned healthcare establishments avoid these extensive follow-up procedures because they are part of the original surgery and thus non-billable. Follow-up interviews do not increase their bottom line, their revenue, and their profits. The key difference is this: patient complications are considered additional revenue to privately-owned hospitals, whereas, to the VA, the same complications are considered as additional, unnecessary, and avoidable cost.

During the veteran's recovery, twice the veteran called a 24/7 nurse helpline to have medical questions answered and Yes, the vet spoke to a real person.

In privately-owned healthcare, do patients have access to a 24/7 medical helpline?

The VA provides this service primarily to save money, but it also has the secondary effect of improving the patient's quality of care by identifying the veteran's healthcare problems before these problems become acute, difficult, and more expensive to treat.

In addition, the VA provides the website, myhealth.va.gov, an online healthcare program for veterans[24]. This easy-to-use, web-based, online system allows patients to review lab test results, appointments, doctors' notes, prescriptions, and wellness reminders ranging from flu shots to weight management. Veterans are actively informed, encouraged, and counseled to use the website to actively take control of their own healthcare and wellbeing. This serves as an effective preventive healthcare measure to monitor, discover, and catch healthcare problems earlier rather than later and to mitigate some of the workload placed upon the VA healthcare professionals.

As a comparison, in the privately-owned healthcare in a study conducted on the implementation of online healthcare services, they found that older demographics, the ones typically suffering from chronic ailments and in need of persistent, continuous, and repeated healthcare, were either unaware of the existence of such services or found them difficult to use according to the National Institutes of Health[25].

Appallingly, in another study the not so bold idea of allowing patients to view their doctors' notes was tested for viability, feasibility, and potentiality. Of the over 13,000 patients involved, over 11,000, or 84%

opened such notes to interface with doctors and to understand their healthcare in more depth reported by the National Center for Biotechnology Information and found in the National Library of Medicine[26]. This shows that patients have a strong interest in their healthcare and are highly likely to take advantage of the online, web-based, patient healthcare portal like the VA's myhealth.va.gov. Unfortunately, non-veterans do not have access to a life-saving and preventative healthcare information system which identifies, prevents, and mitigates illnesses earlier rather than later. Thus, healthcare costs become less expensive rather than more expensive. However, as this was just an experiment, the widespread application of this two-way communication between doctors and patients is severely lacking in the privately-owned healthcare sector.

Complementing the virtual aspects of healthcare, the VA sends medicine to veterans via mail and refills are secured via telephone calls or online.

Is one's medicine sent to one's home?

Fortunately, pharmacies such as CVS, Walgreens, and Walmart now offer mail services for medication to cover up to 90 days' worth of prescriptions according to the National Institutes of Health[27].

The VA has nurses working on the National VA healthcare line. These nurses gather information via the patients' phone interviews. With this patient information and the VA national medical protocols, procedures, and practices, the nurse makes a medical recommendation to the veteran.

An example is as follows:

A veteran's ladder collapsed and fell to the ground, causing a collision and an injury to the vet's head. For a brief period, the veteran was knocked unconscious. The veteran regained consciousness. The veteran felt disoriented but otherwise unaffected by the head collision. The veteran called the National VA health line. The nurse determined quickly, accurately, and appropriately that the patient needed to go to the VA Emergency Room and undergo an MRI of the brain to ensure that there were no internal brain injuries such as bleeding, hemorrhaging, or fluid buildup. In this example, even though the veteran was not suffering from any obvious injury, the VA recognized that injuries caught early are less complicated to address and, of course, less costly to treat. A call was placed to the veteran's emergency room providing information on the veteran's medical condition and healthcare needs.

Does privately-owned healthcare provide a national healthcare line to provide medical information, healthcare guidance to patients, and healthcare information to healthcare providers?

Privately-owned healthcare would lose revenue if they managed injuries, like the VA currently does, before these injuries become acute, severe, and serious.

The VA is the largest integrated health-care system in the U.S. as cited in Veterans Health Administration.[28] With their size, the VA negotiates bulk prices for medical equipment, medical supplies, and pharmaceutical medicine. An example is the VA's average cost per prescription is $28, whereas Medicaid's average cost per prescription $40. This is a savings of 30% cited in "Pharmaceutical Costs: A Comparison of Department of Veterans Affairs (VA), Medicaid, and Medicare Policies"[29] The fragmented privately-owned healthcare industry does not have this extremely large bulk purchasing leverage and power and thus cannot significantly negotiate to reduce medical expenses.

The VA integrated healthcare software maintains detailed patient information and is available to all 1,270 VA medical facilities and to any VA healthcare provider in the U.S. This allows the VA patient to travel virtually anywhere in the U.S. with the peace of mind that they will receive consistent, appropriate, and continuous healthcare, regardless of their location. In the event of an emergency, the VA patients' medical records are available and reduce medical mistakes. In the privately-owned healthcare industry, information is so fragmented that it creates problems, concerns, and apprehension for those who want to visit, travel, or move to other locations in the U.S. Without a universal system, medical records that may be easily accessed in one's hometown may be all but unreachable, unavailable, and unusable for hospital across country, state, or even county lines. This presents the risk that while traveling, one may receive improper healthcare.

Does privately-owned healthcare systems allow for patients' healthcare information to seamlessly be available when patients are traveling and not near their local privately-owned healthcare?

The VA has the most extensive, largest, and comprehensive DNA medical research studies in the world. Over a million veterans have allowed the VA to use their DNA to better understand the veterans' health history[30] as reported by the VA office of Research & Development. This study enables the VA to identify, based on DNA profile, the propensity for illnesses and chronic health conditions before they become acute, known, symptomatic, or indicative. This VA preventive healthcare is just another example of how the VA reduces medical expenditures and keeps VA patients healthier. The privately-owned healthcare industry does not have this extensive DNA database for identifying DNA markers associated with illnesses or chronic health conditions.

As a result of this study, VA has recently discovered three genes, PDE3B, PCSK9, and ANGPTL4, that control levels of cholesterol. With this discovery, new drugs and new treatments will be developed to reduce diabetes, cardiovascular diseases, heart disease, and abdominal aortic aneurysms.

Pg. 34

"This is fantastic news, not just for Veterans, but for all Americans suffering from these diseases," said Former VA Secretary Robert Wilkie. "VA researchers have been improving the lives of Veterans and all Americans through healthcare discovery and innovation for decades. Their groundbreaking research has resulted in three Nobel prizes and numerous other national and international honors."[31]

Did one's privately-owned healthcare receive a Nobel prize for groundbreaking healthcare discoveries?

The Vantage Point identifies the VA's Nobel Prizes.[32]

VA created an artificial lung that will revolutionize lung disease treatment.

"Our Veterans deserve the highest quality of care and the latest breakthroughs in medical science," said former VA Secretary, Robert Wilkie. "This exciting project is the latest in a long string of incredible research and medical advancements developed by VA researchers over the years. The results of this project could change millions of lives for the better."[33] This was reported by the VA's Office of Public and Intergovernmental Affairs.

During a ten-year period from 1990 – 2000, private healthcare costs had increased by 74% as found in the Health System Tracker[34] while VA healthcare costs had increased by only 33% as cited in VA: Historical Budget Authority, FY1940-FY2012.[35] During that same period, healthcare at VA hospitals has improved while patient loads have grown as a result of the 1990 Invasion of Panama, 1990 Gulf War, 1992 U.S. Intervention in Somali, 1992 Bosnian War, 1994 Intervention in Haiti, 1998 Kosovo War and 1998 Operation Infinite Reach.

The VA healthcare providers are paid a salary and generally have 25-30 minutes to perform a standard examination. The VA healthcare providers listen and welcome questions from the veteran. The VA appointments are punctual and almost always start on time. In the privately-owned healthcare system, one may wait for 2 or more hours for a 5-minute medical exam. This problem is so rampant in the private sector, that it has become common practice for patients to take measures to reduce their wait times (see image below).

Generally, the privately-owned healthcare examinations last only 5 minutes and if the patient is lucky, 15 minutes. This short exam time is motivated by increased revenue and profits since the privately-owned healthcare providers are paid the same for this billable event, the exam, regardless, if the patient exam lasts 5 minutes or 25 minutes. In the privately-owned healthcare industry, the patient's questions are not welcome and frowned on by the privately-owned healthcare providers.

How long was one's wait in the medical waiting area? How long did the healthcare examination last?

According to Very Well Health, a doctor's income is based on the number of patients and procedures performed regardless of the time spent.[36] Physicians are instructed to base examine billing codes not on time spent according to Family Practice Management.[37]

Are one's healthcare questions welcomed and answered?

The VA maintains the largest and the most comprehensive database of sound, effective, and efficient medical treatments, protocols, and procedures. The VA's medical protocols have efficacy and are shown to work. The privately-owned healthcare protocols do not exist or are so fragmented as to be of little use.

Even with a 24% lower healthcare cost, the VA health statistics, medical care, and patient loyalty are significantly better than the privately-owned healthcare industry.

Federal HMOs

Based on the VA Model, a Free Choice Market Solution

Using the VA healthcare model, the federal government would set up Federal HMOs across the United States. Through the free market choice, the patient and not the government would decide whether to seek medical care at the Federal HMOs or at the privately-owned HMOs.

Federal HMOs would benefit from the VA's infrastructure, medical protocols, and discounted purchasing power to reduce the healthcare cost by 40% to 50% over privately-owned HMO's. Initially, the Federal HMOs would be set up and created in one or two major cities. If through the patients' free market choice, these Federal HMOs are successful, then Federal HMOs would be created in other major cities and eventually spread across the nation.

Misleading Arguments Against Federal HMO's

The VA has unfair advantages over privately-owned HMOs.

The government does not need to charge more than the actual cost of healthcare. Privately-owned HMOs charge 20% to 30% more to create income for executives, shareholders, and investors. 20% to 30%

of income paid to these executives, shareholders, and investors do not result in better healthcare at lower costs to patients. The Federal HMOs' advantage is that it would benefit from the VA's purchasing power, infrastructure, protocols, procedures, wellness programs, and healthcare advances.

Should the VA apologize for providing less expensive and better healthcare than the privately-owned healthcare can deliver?

VA has problems with healthcare for Veterans.

The privately-owned healthcare spends large amounts of money identifying, highlighting, exaggerating, and lying about VA problems. The privately-owned healthcare will never address and overcome the problematic issues in the privately-owned healthcare industry:

- The 3rd highest cause of death is medical mistakes,
- Over 250,000 die each year because of healthcare providers' medical errs,
- The fragmented and spotty privately-owned healthcare and
- The lack of financial incentive to prevent illnesses, to reduce the need for acute expensive medical care, and to keep patients healthy.

VA patients consistently rate their medical care higher than privately-owned healthcare patients rate their healthcare.

The Federal HMOs will cause unemployment to rise for privately-owned healthcare providers.

The Federal HMOs will require healthcare providers: doctors, nurses, specialists, technicians, etc. Since these skills are transferable, many healthcare professionals will be hired from the privately-owned HMOs to operate the Federal HMOs. Many of these privately-owned HMOs' healthcare providers will gravitate to Federal HMOs where healthcare means keeping the patient healthy versus exploiting sicknesses, illnesses, and injuries to generate additional income and profit.

Global Purchasing Prescription Drugs Act (GPPDA)

Currently, it is illegal to buy prescription medicine directly from other countries that manufacture prescription drugs for the U.S. The countries that manufacture prescription drugs sold in the U.S. include Australia, Canada, China, India, France, Germany, Japan, Malta, Singapore, Sweden, and the United Kingdom[38] according to Pharmacy Checker.com. The Global Purchasing Prescription Drugs Act (GPPDA) would allow Americans to purchase prescription drugs directly from other countries. GPPDA would result in a savings of 40% to 60% for prescription drugs.

The U.S. pays:
- *Three times more for prescription medicine than Britain,*
- *Six times higher than in Brazil and*
- *16 times higher than in India.[39]*

According to Scientific American as reported by Reuters.

False and Misleading Arguments:

Safety and Purity of Medicine require that medicine be purchased only in the U.S.

This is a false argument since many prescription drugs are manufactured in other countries but sold in the U.S. Patients' direct purchasing of these medicine from FDA approved foreign manufacturers would eliminate the mark-up costs of importers, wholesale outlets, distributors, and drug stores.

Do Americans want to buy medicine at lower prices? Yes! Of Course!

Medical research for newer and better medicine will be substantially reduced.

This is false, dishonest, and misleading. The federal and state governments along with philanthropic organizations fund the lion share of the cost of the research and the discovery of medical drugs[40] as reported by the National Academy of Sciences. Pharmaceutical companies and venture capitalists do not pay for the research, the development, and the discovery of medical drugs. However, pharmaceutical companies and venture capitalists conduct studies and market the medical drugs for which they have not paid for the research, the development, and the discovery.

Could the licensing by government and philanthropic organizations of their discovered medical drugs create additional revenue for the funding of future medical drugs? Maybe, Probably, Likely, Surely.

Could this be a self-funding (no taxpayers' money) for even better medical research of drugs which would have the potential of creating the newest and the best medical drugs in the world?

Preventive Healthcare Act (PHA)

In the U.S., preventive medicine is not a priority for privately-owned healthcare. The privately-owned healthcare income is reduced when the occurrences of illnesses and diseases are reduced or prevented. When CDC interviewed healthcare professionals about preventative medicine, the issue of finances was always brought up. One interviewee said "If there is no margin, there is no mission"[41] This implies that if an action pays no dividends, then it is a waste of resources for the private healthcare sector to pursue. Preventive medicine is a priority at the VA. By reducing or eliminating illnesses and diseases, the VA saves money.

In the U.S., preventive healthcare can become the norm, and, in doing so, reduce the high costs of healthcare. These healthcare costs include copays, deductibles, and co-insurance. For instance, addressing high blood pressure, an easily managed symptom with proper consultation and modifications to diet, exercise, and medication alone can save over $55 billion in medications, medical services, and missed work[42] according to the CDC.

From HeathCare.gov, preventative healthcare measures include:[43]

1. Abdominal aortic aneurysm one-time screening for men of specified ages who have ever smoked,

2. Alcohol misuse screening and counseling,
3. Aspirin use to prevent cardiovascular disease and colorectal cancer for adults 50 to 59 years old with a high cardiovascular risk,
4. Blood pressure screening,
5. Cholesterol screening for adults of certain ages or at higher risk,
6. Colorectal cancer screening for adults 50 to 75 years old,
7. Depression screening.
8. Diabetes (Type 2) screening for adults 40 to 70 years old who are overweight or obese,
9. Diet counseling for adults at higher risk for chronic diseases,
10. Falls prevention (with exercise or physical therapy and vitamin D) for adults 65 years and older, living in a community setting,
11. Hepatitis B screening for people at high risk, including people from countries with 2% or more Hepatitis B prevalence, and U.S. born people not vaccinated as infants and with at least one parent born in a region with 8% or more Hepatitis B prevalence,
12. Hepatitis C screening for adults at increased risk, and one-time for everyone born between 1945 and 1965.
13. HIV screening for everyone ages 15 to 65, and other ages at increased risk,
14. Immunization vaccines for adults — doses, recommended ages, and recommended populations vary. The following are diseases for which vaccines exist:

    o   Diphtheria
    o   Hepatitis A

- o Hepatitis B
- o Herpes Zoster
- o Human Papillomavirus (HPV)
- o Influenza (flu shot)
- o Measles
- o Meningococcal
- o Mumps
- o Pertussis
- o Pneumococcal
- o Rubella
- o Tetanus
- o Varicella (Chickenpox)

15. Lung cancer screening for adults 55 to 80 years old who are at high risk for lung cancer because they're heavy smokers or have quit in the past 15 years,
16. Obesity screening and counseling,
17. Sexually transmitted infection (STI) prevention counseling for adults at higher risk,
18. Statin preventive medication for adults 40 to 75 years old and at high risk,
19. Syphilis screening for adults at higher risk,
20. Tobacco use screening for all adults and cessation interventions for tobacco users,
21. Tuberculosis screening for selected adults without symptoms at high risk.

Reducing Unnecessary Healthcare Act (RUHA),

The Journal of the American Medical Association, (JAMA) reported that more than 20% of healthcare is unnecessary. Fearing lawsuits, doctors stated that "defensive medicine" is the reason for this unnecessary healthcare. Only 3% of healthcare cost is attributable to "defensive medicine." This unnecessary medical care is estimated to cost $765 billion per year[44] according to the JAMA's article, "The High Cost of Unnecessary Care. The VA does not have this enormous problem with unnecessary medical care. The VA has established a medical protocol database based on the need, the efficacy, and the effectiveness of the healthcare. The privately-owned healthcare does not have this effective medical protocol database. Unnecessary healthcare is additional revenue and profit for the privately-owned healthcare.

U.S. Expensive Healthcare's Poor Results

In many areas, privately-owned businesses perform better than governmental agencies. The healthcare industry is an exception. The privately-owned healthcare system is:

- where revenue is churned out at the expense of the health of patients,
- where a sick society results in more revenue than a healthy community,
- where nurses, doctors, and other healthcare workers are overworked to increase revenue,
- where many are unable to afford preventive healthcare, increasing the cost of healthcare and reducing the results of healthcare,
- where poor medical care results in medical complications and increases revenue and
- where healthcare professionals are paid based on a fee for services and not for results.

The following information and charts come from The Commonwealth Fund.[45]

Exhibit 1. Health Care Spending as a Percentage of GDP, 1980–2013

* 2012.

Notes: GDP refers to gross domestic product. Dutch and Swiss data are for current spending only, and exclude spending on capital formation of health care providers.
Source: OECD Health Data 2015.

The U.S. is at the bottom or near the bottom in health statistics of the 13 reported countries. In healthcare spending as a percentage of Gross Domestic Product, GDP, the U.S. spends nearly double the GDP percentage as compared to the average for the other 12 countries. The U.S. spends 17% of GDP as compared to the 12 other countries who spend on average 10.5% of their GDP on healthcare.

Exhibit 2. Health Care Spending, 2013

	Total health care spending per capita[e]	Real average annual growth rate per capita		Current health care spending per capita, by source of financing[e,f]		
					Private	
		2003-2009	2009-2013	Public	Out-of-pocket	Other
Australia	$4,115[a]	2.70%	2.42%[c]	$2,614[a]	$771[a]	$480[a]
Canada	$4,569	3.15%	0.22%	$3,074	$623	$654
Denmark	$4,847	3.32%	-0.17%	$3,841	$625	$88
France	$4,361	1.72%	1.35%	$3,247	$277	$600
Germany	$4,920	2.01%	1.95%	$3,677	$649	$492
Japan	$3,713	3.08%	3.83%	$2,965[a]	$503[a]	$124[a]
Netherlands	$5,131[d]	4.75%[d]	1.73%[d]	$4,495	$270	$366
New Zealand	$3,855	6.11%[b]	0.82%	$2,656	$420	$251
Norway	$6,170	1.59%	1.40%	$4,981	$855	$26
Sweden	$5,153	1.82%[d]	6.95%[d]	$4,126	$726	$53
Switzerland	$6,325[d]	1.42%[d]	2.54%[d]	$4,178	$1,630	$454
United Kingdom	$3,364	4.00%	-0.88%	$2,802	$321	$240
United States[e]	$9,086	2.47%	1.50%	$4,197	$1,074	$3,442
OECD median	$3,661	3.10%	1.24%	$2,598	$625	$181

[a] 2012. [b] 2002-2009. [c] 2009-2012.
[d] Current spending only; excludes spending on capital formation of health care providers.
[e] Adjusted for differences in the cost of living.
[f] Numbers may not sum to total health care spending per capita due to excluding capital formation of health care providers, and some uncategorized spending.
Source: OECD Health Data 2015.

The U.S. spends $9,086 per capita on healthcare, whereas. the other 12 countries average per capita healthcare spending is nearly half that at $4,710.25 per capita. All the countries above apart from the U.S. provide universal healthcare. Universal healthcare is a healthcare system where every legal resident has primary healthcare. These countries can provide 100% of their legal residents with healthcare at 50% of healthcare cost in the U.S. In the U.S., 44 million people or 13% of the U.S. population have no healthcare insurance. If one sees a group of ten people, at least one will not have healthcare insurance. This lack of healthcare in the U.S. contributes to poor healthcare statistics as compared to other countries. Employer-sponsored healthcare cost is tax deductible. The U.S. healthcare cost of $9,086 per capita ignores this employer-sponsored health insurance tax benefits, which is about $250 billion per year, which is an additional healthcare cost. The inclusion of the employer healthcare tax benefit increases the U.S. healthcare cost per capita to $9800.

The soaring U.S. healthcare begs the question as to *WHY.*

The U.S. privately-owned healthcare stresses profits over health, whereas the VA and the countries with universal healthcare stress health and preventative healthcare to reduce costs.

The following countries provide universal healthcare for their residents[46] according to the New York Department of Health:

Country	Started
Australia	1975
Austria	1967
Bahrain	1957
Belgium	1945
Brunei	1958
Canada	1966
Cyprus	1980
Denmark	1973
Finland	1972
France	1974

Germany	1941
Greece	1983
Hong Kong	1993
Iceland	1990
Ireland	1977
Israel	1995
Italy	1978
Japan	1938
Kuwait	1950
Luxembourg	1973
Netherlands	1966
New Zealand	1938
Norway	1912
Portugal	1979
Singapore	1993
Slovenia	1972
South Korea	1988
Spain	1986
Sweden	1955
Switzerland	1994
United Arab Emirates	1971
United Kingdom	1948

Hospital and physician prices in the U.S. are the highest in the world. Bypass Surgery in the U.S. costs on average $75,345 as compared to $33,687 average for the other countries. Appendectomy in the U.S. cost $13,910 as compared to $6,666 average for the other countries. An MRI scan in the U.S. cost $1,145 as compared to $488 average for the other countries. CT scan in the U.S. cost $896 as compared to $407 average for the other countries. Pharmaceuticals in the U.S. cost $199 as compared to $64 average for the other countries[47] according to Health System Tracker.

Life expectancy in the U.S. is 78.8 years as compared to the average for the other countries of 81.8 years. The percent with 2 or more chronic conditions in the U.S. is 68% as compared to the average for the other countries of 44.7%.

The following information is from the website America's Health Ranking as compared to 35 other countries.[48]

The U.S. healthcare rankings and statistics:

- The U.S. ranks near the bottom of Infant Deaths, 29th out of 35 countries. In school, being at the bottom 1/6th of a class would be considered failing.
- The U.S. ranks 26th in life expectancy out of 35 countries.

Although the U.S. ranks near the bottom of all health statics, it ranks by far as the most expensive healthcare in the world.

Are we getting high-quality healthcare at a reasonable price? No!!!!!

Why is the U.S. healthcare system nearly at the bottom of all other countries?

There is *less revenue in a healthy society.* In the U.S. privately-owned healthcare institutions only experience increased revenue when people are sick, not when people are well. Privately-owned healthcare providers are paid based on "Fee for Services". "Fees for Services" are billable procedures such as exams, medical tests, surgical procedures, etc. The "Fee for Services" are the reasons why privately-owned doctors spend so little time examining their patients, 5 minutes, and if the patient is lucky, 15 minutes. No matter how much time the privately-owned healthcare provider spends on exams, the "Fee for Services" are the same. These abbreviated medical exams create medical errs.

Why does Canada pay less for Doctors and still has four times the number of Doctors per 1000 people than the U.S.?

In Canada, there are 1.2 Primary Care Physicians per 1000 people. In the U.S., there are only .3 Primary Care Physicians per 1000 people. Yet, doctors in the U.S. make $55,000 more than Canada doctors. Canada attracts and keeps four times the physicians per 1000 people than the U.S. The relative U.S. shortages of doctors explain why it is so hard to get medical appointments[49] reported in the New York Times.

Why do doctors work for less pay in Canada than in the U.S.?

- *Is it because in Canada, keeping patients healthy, is the goal?*
- *Is it because Canadian physicians feel that patient health is more rewarding than an additional $55,000?*

The U.S. has fewer practicing physicians per 1,000 people than 23 of the 28 countries that reported data in 2013 among nations in the Organization for Economic Cooperation and Development[50] reported in the New York Times.

Given the "Law of Supply and Demand" and the U.S. doctors' incomes are the highest in the world, it is difficult to understand why there is a shortage of doctors in the U.S. The Association of American Medical Colleges predicts there will be a shortage of 90,000 physicians by 2025. Over 3 million people will not have a doctor[51] reported by CNBC's Health and Science article "Doctor shortages: Here's the real culprit."

To address this shortage of doctors, the U.S. needs to increase the number of medical schools, reduce the tuition for medical schools from the staggering median medical school tuition of over $170,000, and increase the number of residency hospitals.

"Medical-school applicants basically need to have near-perfect GPA and very high MCAT scores to get accepted to an accredited U.S. institution. Even among that much better-qualified pool of applicants, only about 50 percent get accepted. Imagine if only half of our high-school grads who applied for college got into any college — there would be riots at the admissions offices every spring." [52] quoted CNBC's Health and Science article "Doctor shortages: Here's the real culprit."

The privately-owned healthcare system uses overcharges, overtreatments, and overuse of unnecessary and needless healthcare to increase revenue, to increase profits, and tragically to increase the cost of healthcare. Almost 1/3 of all U.S. healthcare costs are not necessary. Of the $2.6 trillion spent on healthcare in the U.S., the U.S. wasted $750 billion on unneeded healthcare. The justification is that the extra healthcare procedures, exams, and tests protect privately-owned healthcare providers from lawsuits. Many accept that logic and blame those who sue doctors for the high cost of healthcare. The greed of privately-owned healthcare providers causes many of them to order unnecessary healthcare.

Many believe that medical lawsuits are just attempts to get something for nothing. *Suing healthcare providers is extremely difficult.* From WebMD 5% of doctors are responsible for over 50% of all lawsuits.[53] Preventing these 5% from practicing medicine will reduce the medical malpractice lawsuits by 50%. Doctors know these incompetent doctors and need to report the medical malpractice by these incompetent doctors. The medical community should ban these incompetent doctors from practicing medicine. The medical community should eliminate the Medical *White Code of Silence.*

There exists a database, the National Practitioner Data Base which assembles, collects, reveals, and discloses, negative information on healthcare practitioners': losses of licenses, prohibitions from practicing in Medicare and Medicaid or malpractice awards against the healthcare providers. Healthcare and medical malpractices insurance companies use this database to screen, to avoid hiring and to not insurance these 5% problematic, incompetent, and dangerous healthcare providers. Although public tax dollars fund and pay for this database, this life-saving information is not available to the public. Releasing this information to taxpayers that paid for the National Practitioner Data Base will reduce medical malpractice and improve healthcare in the U.S. by allowing patients to identify and avoid incompetent healthcare providers[54] according to the National Public Radio (NPR) article, "Medical Errors Are No. 3 Cause Of U.S Deaths, Researchers Say."

U.S. Privately-owned Healthcare is Broken.

Conclusion

Most developed countries have realized that to be globally competitive in the world market, their population needs to be healthy. Until there is profit in having a healthy society for privately-owned healthcare providers, this will not occur under the current system. The high healthcare cost in the U.S. acts as an economic drag, anchor, and obstacle on the quality of lives of Americans. It reduces employment and income for every American and every American business. By promoting preventative healthcare measures, using global purchasing power, and passing laws like Medicare Free Choice Act (MFCA) and the Federal Health Maintenance Organization Act (FHMO), the high costs of healthcare in the United States can be drastically, substantially, and extensively reduced while improving American's health.

Making Healthcare Better and Cheaper

Voters Like You need:

- To vote for a president who supports a better and less expensive healthcare,
- To choose a president who creates a whitehouse.gov page that identifies Senators and House Representatives who support,
    - *Medicare Free Choice Act,*
    - *Federal Health Maintenance Organization Act,*
    - *Global Purchasing Prescription Drugs Act,*
    - *Preventive Healthcare Act,* and
    - *Reducing Unnecessary Healthcare Act,*
- To vote for and to elect Senators and Representatives at both the federal and state level that support these congressional federal acts so that healthcare becomes better and less expensive.

Applying Political Pressure for better and less expensive healthcare will be accomplished by:

- Voting,
- Telephoning your Congressional Representatives and your Senators,

- Writing to your Congressional Representatives and your Senators,
- Emailing your Congressional Representatives and your Senators,
- Visiting your Congressional Representatives' and your Senator's offices in your state,
- Visiting your Congressional Representatives' and your Senator's offices in Washington DC,
- Attending your Congressional Representatives' and your Senator's locally held town halls,
- Lobbying of your Congressional Representatives and your Senators,
- Marching and demonstrating,
- Calling political talk radio stations,
- Donating to Congressional Representatives and Senators who support these healthcare acts,
- Volunteering in Congressional Representatives' and Senators' campaigns, and
- Voting for politicians that want better and less expensive healthcare.

Through the actions above by *Voters Like You*, a better and less expensive healthcare will become a reality.

Chapter 2: Shared Economics Increases Pay and Profits

The definition of wealth is having money and property that exceeds the expenses, expenditures, and costs of basic human needs. Basic human needs include food, shelter, clothing, sanitation, education, and healthcare. Wealth is accumulated by one's work or by one's ability to take the wealth of others. Wealth is admired as successes, accomplishments, and class statuses. Wealth can be used to improve the lives of humans or can be used to bring harm, destruction, and damage to humans.

How does one create wealth?

Examples, illustrations, and occurrences of wealth creation are excellent ways to understand how wealth is produced, built, and made.

- Carpenters use lumber to build house frames. The carpenters have increased the value of stacks of lumber into house frames.
- Chefs or cooks use fruits, vegetables, spices, etc. to create and cook edible, delectable, and palatable meals. The chefs or cooks have increased the value of raw food ingredients into edible meals.

- Services provided by doctors, nurses, healthcare providers, lawyers, servers, teachers, etc. are examples of created wealth.
- Scientists or inventors create new inventions or scientific findings that improve the lives of others and have created wealth.
- The list of wealth creators is exceptionally long. Please excuse the omission of one's profession or work.
- Simply put, workers through their labors create wealth by producing products or providing services.

Wealth Creators

Create Products

Provide Services

The employees create wealth through their labors.
The business investors and owners who do not share
this wealth with their employees are missing a
golden, gigantic, and huge opportunity to increase
business profits by 50%. This is counter intuitive that
the businesses who pay employees the lowest

possible wages create less profit and income. Whereas, profit sharing, the Shared Capitalism model of splitting profits between employees and businesses increases businesses' profits by 50%.

Shared Capitalism is the sharing of the wealth created by the laborers of workers with the employees and the business owners. The current economic model, the relationship between the business owners, and the employees are that the business owners pay the employees as little as possible and take nearly all the employees' labors created wealth.

Shared Capitalism is where the wealth created by employees' labors are shared equally between employees and business owners. History has clearly shown that *Shared Capitalism* cannot be dictated, legislated, or forced. But it can happen by appealing to the desires and wishes of the business owners to increase their profits by 50%. It may seem nonsensical, illogical, or implausible that those business owners who employ *Shared Capitalism* will increase their wealth by over 50%. Is it possible that the business owners who do not apply *Shared Capitalism* will experience a reduction in their wealth and may even suffer bankruptcy resulting in the complete loss and destruction of their businesses?

The current economics where the business owners do not share employees' created wealth has reduced by 50% the amount of wealth that those business owners could have under *Shared Capitalism*.

Shared Capitalism Versus Current Capitalism:

- Under *Shared Capitalism*, employees are 40% more productive when they are incentivized by the profit motive and thus, receive ½ of the profit that they help create.
- Under *Shared Capitalism*, supervisors are less likely to be needed to oversee the work of the employees, which represents a savings or reduction in total wages and cost of 20%. Think of one's experience with supervisors who have no clue how to do employees' work, who have never done the employees' work, who probably could not do the employees' work, and who have pushed employees to work harder and faster to the brink of employees' insanity.
- Under the *Current Capitalism*, it is a game between the employees doing as little as possible and the business owners demanding as much as possible.
- Under *Shared Capitalism*, employees have a more significant, improved, and better incentives, desires, and motivations to work faster, to work harder, to work smarter, to work safer, to work with more care, and to work more efficiently. *Shared Capitalism* increases employees' production by 40%.

- Under *Shared Capitalism*, employees are motivated, incentivized, and driven to handle with great care the company's equipment, machines, vehicles, etc. *Shared Capitalism* saves the company between 5% to 10% in equipment repairs.
- Under the *Current Capitalism*, employees who are just paid a wage have no incentive to work harder or to take better care of the company's equipment, machines, vehicles, etc. resulting in lost profits.
- Under the *Current Capitalism*, when a company's equipment, machines, or vehicles break down, employees are not productive and are paid for their time while repairs are made.
- Under *Shared Capitalism*, companies save on unnecessary repairs and employees' downtime. This can be additional savings of between 5% and 10%.
- Companies who use, employ, or practice *Shared Capitalism* will attract better and superior workers than companies who do not apply, utilize, or practice *Shared Capitalism*.
- The employees will always seek better compensation for their labors. This increase in the quality of employees makes the business owners more profits.
- Under *Shared Capitalism*, better employees perform at levels of 10% to 30% higher.
- Under *Current Capitalism,* customer service and treatment are inferior and indifferent. *Were the retail clerks' treatments of*

customers, friendly, helpful, and energetic projecting enthusiasm? Or were the clerks' customer interfaces indifferent, ineffective, and lethargic with a ballooning air of annoyed indifference?

- Under *Shared Capitalism*, employees are incentivized and motivated to treat customers better because that creates more wealth for themselves.
- Under *Shared Capitalism*, this better and improved customer service interfaces will add an additional 5% to 10% to the company's profit.
- Customers will shop and buy products and services from companies where the customers are treated the best.
- *If cost and services are similar between companies where some companies employ Shared Capitalism and other businesses remain with Current Capitalism, will customers shop and buy products and services where customers are treated as important, as desired, as unique and with great respect?*
- Under *Shared Capitalism*, the employees realize that the more they produce and the better they treat customers, the more profits they will earn.
- Under *Shared Capitalism*, the employees are motivated to do their work right when no one is looking.

Business Profits Increase by 50%

The following example demonstrates, explains, and describes how *Shared Capitalism* works.

- Company A's annual gross revenue is $100 million, with a profit of $20 million. Of course, under the *Current Capitalism* model, the $20 million in profit would not be shared with the employees.
- Under *Shared Capitalism* the employees would receive ½ of the profits or $10 million.
- The ½ of the profits or $10 million is shared on a prorated basis of a worker's or employee's pay or salary as compared to the wages or salaries of all the other employees.
- Assume that the total payroll for Company A is $10 million and that an employee is paid $75,000 per year. That employee would receive an additional $75,000. In fact, all employees would double their pay.

Under *Shared Capitalism*, the employees realize that the more they produce, the more careful that they are with the companies' equipment, vehicles, and machines, and the better that they are with customers' interfaces, the more profits they earn. With profit sharing, the employees are likely to be 40% more productive and incentivize to work faster, harder, safer, and smarter. The employer will no longer need supervisors to ensure that employees are working. Henry Ford is quoted "*Doing the right thing when no one is looking.*"[55] This is a reduction of supervisors' payroll of $2 million or an increase in Company A's profit of $2 million.

Under *Shared Capitalism*, Company A's annual gross revenue increases to at least $140 million, 40% higher than the $100 million under *Current Capitalism*. Company A's fixed cost, which includes depreciation, insurance, interest, rent, salaries, and wages remains virtually unchanged irrespective of the 40% increase in products or services. Company A's incremental cost, the cost of producing additional products or services to include material, electricity, etc. is negligible, insignificant, and tiny. Company A's profit is now $60 million under Shared Capitalism rather than the $20 million under *Current Capitalism*. This $60 million includes the original $20 million profit under today's economics plus the additional $40 million under *Shared Capitalism*. ½ of the $60 million, $30 million remains with the business owners, and $30 million is shared with the employees. Therefore, under *Shared Capitalism*, the business owners would receive 50% more or $10 million. The business owners' profit increased from $20 million under *Current Capitalism* to $30 million under *Shared Capitalism*.

Shared Capitalism has a historical precedent, a past example, that clearly demonstrates that *Shared Capitalism* works.

Henry Ford's Shared Capitalism

Henry Ford

Awarded 161 Patents
Father of the Assembly Line
Founder of Ford Motor Company
"Quality means doing right
when no one is looking!!"

In 1914, Henry Ford, the founder of Ford Motor Company, used a form of *Shared Capitalism* to dominate the manufacturing of automobiles.

In 1914, auto manufacturers reduced the wages of their employees to the lowest possible. In 1914, Henry Ford doubled his employees' wages, twice what other auto manufacturers paid their employees and reduced the workday by 50% from 12 hours to 8 hours. The increase in wages and the reduction in hours combined increasing Ford's employees' wages per hour by 300%.

Economists, newspapers, other auto companies, and even Ford Motor Executives working for Henry Ford thought Henry Ford was crazy and that it would bust the Ford Motor Company. The business owners had the arrogance, hubris, and decadence to suggest that Ford employees would be "demoralized by this sudden affluence." This sudden affluence refers to the increase in employees' wages.

Really?

Would any employee genuinely become disheartened, depressed, and saddened by having more money for a better life for themselves and their families?

Because of Henry Ford's *Shared Capitalism*.

- The Ford Motor Company kept and hired the best employees, which increased the company's profits.
- Ford employees treated their equipment with additional care, which increased Ford's profits.
- Ford employees required little supervision, which increased the company's profits.
- Ford employees worked harder, faster, and smarter, which increased Ford's profits.
- Henry Ford understood that the assembly line work is monotonous, repetitive, and tedious.
- He realized that an increase in wages and a reduction in working hours would keep and get the best assembly line workers.

In 1914, Ford Motor Company manufactured and sold 308,000 autos. In 1920 and under *Shared Capitalism*, Ford Motor Company produced and sold over a million cars per year. This was more than the combined total of all other auto manufacturers.

Henry Ford stated that the most significant reason to increase wages as written in the book titled "*Today and Tomorrow.*"

- *"The owner, the employees, and the buying public are all the same, and unless the industry can so manage itself as to keep wages high and prices low, it destroys itself, for otherwise, it limits the number of its customers. One's employees ought to be one's own best customers."*
- *"We increased the buying power of our people, and they increased the buying power of other people, etc."* This is the snowball effect.
- *"It is this thought of enlarging buying power by paying high wages and selling at low prices that is behind the prosperity of this country."*

Henry Ford realized that tripling of wages was not an additional expense but was cost-cutting and profit-increasing. Henry Ford continued to increase wages, which continued to reduce expenses and create more profit for the Ford Motor Company. Henry Ford is rumored to have said with a mischievous grin, a mysterious twinkle in his eyes, and a slight laugh, *"The more I pay my employees, the more profit I make"*.

Henry Ford blamed the 1929 Stock Market Crash on business leaders' greed, who were continually putting the profit motive over what he called the wage motive. Henry Ford explained, *"When a business thinks only of profit for the owners instead of providing goods for all, then it frequently broke down.*"[56] During the depression, Henry Ford increased wages by 40% to $7 a day.

Eventually, virtually all auto manufacturers copied and implemented the "Ford Motor's Wage Increase Model for increased productivity and profits.

Henry Ford stated, "*The highest use of capital is not to make more money, but to make money do more for the betterment of life.*" This is *Shared Capitalism*.

But it was too late for some auto manufacturers. The following is a partial list of 1914 auto manufacturers that do not exist today:

- Chalmers (1911–1924)
- Maxwell (1905–1925)
- Cartercar (1906–1916)
- Oakland (1907–1931)
- Scripps Booth (1913–1923)

This is a strong rationale and an argument for why and how Shared Capitalism worked and will work again.

How can Shared Capitalism become a reality?

Initially, just as they did with Henry Ford, the business owners will cast doubts on the viability of *Shared Capitalism* and will discredit *Shared Capitalism*. But some of the business owners will understand the positive effects of *Shared Capitalism* and will enact *Shared Capitalism*. Those first companies to employ *Shared Capitalism* will reap the highest returns by having the best employees, by creating the highest quality products, and having the best customer interfaces, which will allow them to dominate their market. Business owners that are late or fail to enact *Shared Capitalism* will vanish as they did in the 1900s. The defunct and outdated auto companies of the 1900's disappeared because they did not adopt *Shared Capitalism*. The business owners that fail to embrace *Shared Capitalism* risk reduced profits, reduced market shares, slash revenues, increased expenses, bankruptcies, and even going out of business.

Employees with more disposable income will buy more goods and services. This increase in demand for products and services will create more profits for the business owners. These business owners will need to hire more employees to meet the increasing demand for their products or services. This would have a snowball effect increasing the U.S. GDP.

How much of an increase in GDP will depend on how many businesses initiate and employ *Shared Capitalism*?

The current U.S. GDP is about $18 trillion per year. Assuming a profit of 20%, this is $3.6 trillion in profits. Based on the *Shared Capitalism* model above, there would be an increase of $1.8 trillion in profits, an increase of 10% in GDP. Thus, GDP would increase from $18 trillion to $19.8 trillion, an increase of 10% in the GDP. This only includes the additional profits in GDP and not the increase in GDP that would result from the snowball effect of increased wages of employees who would buy more goods and services.

Economic growth under *Shared Capitalism* will exceed the combined annual growth of GDP from the *Demand Side Economics Era* from1940s-1970s which was 4.2 % yearly growth and from *Supply Side Economics Era* beginning in the 1980s to the present which is 2.6% annual GDP growth. How much the annual GDP growth is difficult to determine, but 6.8% annual GDP growth is well within the possibilities.

Why is this prediction possible?

- The employees will be 40% more productive.
- The employees will have extra discretionary funds that are not spent on necessary living expenses, water, electricity, rent or mortgage, transportation to work, food, etc.
- The employees will buy additional goods and services with this increase in wages.
- This increasing demand will increase the need for more employees who will now have money to buy more goods and services.

- This snowball effect will increase the wealth of both the employees and their business owners.

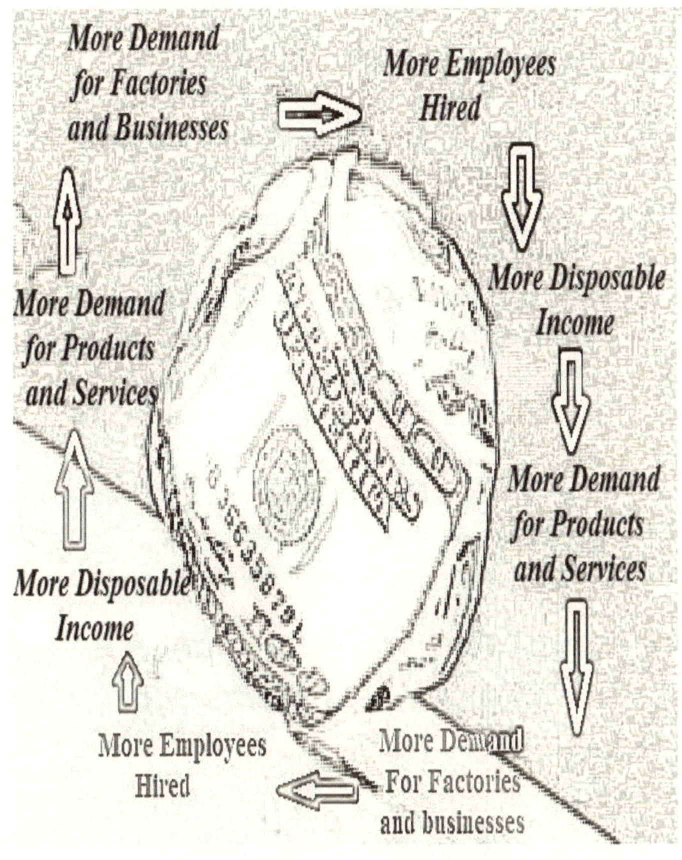

The Shared Capitalism's snowball effect rolls down the hill, collects more snow, the markets, and increases in size, the economy. Thus, wealth is increased for businesses and their employees.

How does Shared Capitalism become a reality replacing current economics?

- Elect a president who believes in the effectiveness and in the fairness of *Shared Capitalism*.
- Elect politicians who supported *Shared Capitalism*.
- The federal government cannot legislate or create laws to compel business owners to share their profits with employees.
- The creation of a Department of Labor webpage identifying companies that share their profits with their employees, the amount of profits, and the percentage of profits shared. This is all that is needed to propel *Shared Capitalism*.
- The best and most productive employees will gravitate to this webpage and seek employment in *Shared Capitalism* companies.

Is it fair and profitable to share the profits that employees create with employees?

Of Course, Yes!!!!

Chapter 3: Taxing Fair and Balance for All

There are two currently recognized distinct capitalists or economic systems: Demand Side Economics and Supply Side Economics. There is a third unrecognized capitalists or economics, Balance Economics. The history, the pros, the cons and the actual effects of Demand Side Economics and Supply Side Economics will be discussed. This will be compared with Balance Economics. *Taxing Fair and Balance for All* results in a tax savings on average of $5,000 for the average taxpayers and an increase in GDP (Gross Domestic Product) of 3.1% to 16%. An increase in GDP benefits all, businesses, the upper class, upper-middle class, middle class, working class, and lower class.

Demand Side Economics 1940 to 1979

The U.S. industries, factories, and businesses mobilized for World War II. President Franklin Roosevelt stated, "Powerful enemies must be out-fought and out-produced." This Word War II mobilization included the creation of more than 100,000 factories. An additional 24 million people worked in these factories producing weapons, aircrafts, tanks, ships, food, uniforms, etc. Most of these 24 million people were females who for the first time worked outside of the home. Household incomes increased dramatically. Thus, people and families had disposable income, income not used for basic essential needs: food, shelter, clothing, sanitation, education, and healthcare. From the 1940's to the 1970's, American workers received the highest and most significant increase in their standard of living in all human history. Families could buy homes, buy cars, pay college tuition for their children, take vacations, etc. This increase in worker disposable income led to an increase in demand for products, services, and consumables. This increased demand for products, services, and goods required companies to expand factories and, thus, hire more workers. U.S. businesses were flush with money to invest in new factories to meet consumers' increased purchasing of goods and services. Companies provided healthcare for their workers. Workers' contributions to healthcare were less than 10% of the cost of healthcare. Today, workers' contributions to their healthcare are more than 29% of the cost of healthcare from the Kaiser Family Foundation's 2016 Employer Health Benefits Survey.[57]

This is the snowball effect. More demand for products and services requires more factories. More factories need more employees who now have better-paying jobs. The increase in good paying jobs creates more disposable income for the average taxpayer. More disposable income increases the demand for products and services known as consumer consumption. Thus, the snowball effect increases the size of the U.S. economy, the Gross Domestic Product (GDP). This period represents the most massive economic growth and prosperity for the U.S., for businesses, the upper class, upper-middle class, middle class, working class, and lower class. President Kennedy famously stated, "A rising tide lifts all boats." As a metaphor, this reflects that an expanding economy benefits all participants in that economy: businesses, the upper class, upper-middle class, middle class, working class, and lower class.

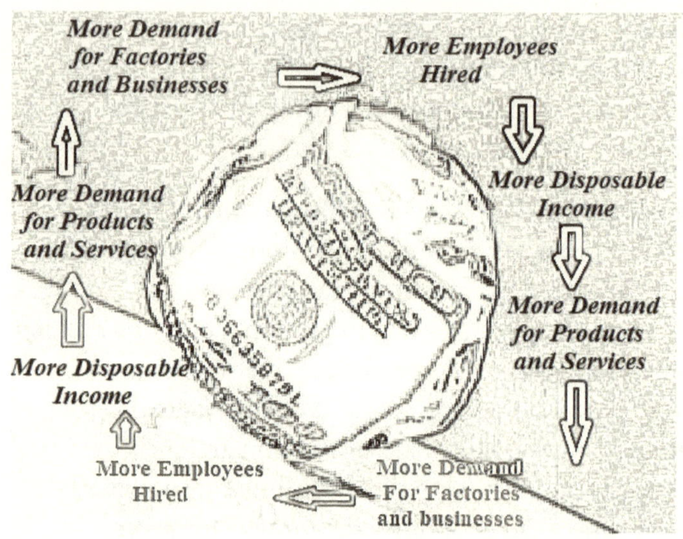

The U.S. cities, counties, states, and federal governments were flush with money. Wisely, the government invested in infrastructure: highways, railways, water, sewer, electrical grid, higher education, etc. The Federal Government provided the means for elders to have a retirement, Social Security, and to have healthcare, Medicare. This was the first time that U.S. workers could retire from work with a retirement and healthcare. The U.S. increased exports to other countries. For this period, "Made in the USA" was a stamp of product excellence, treasured and desired by the rest of the world. Thus, the giant U.S economy dwarfed the economies of every other nation combined.

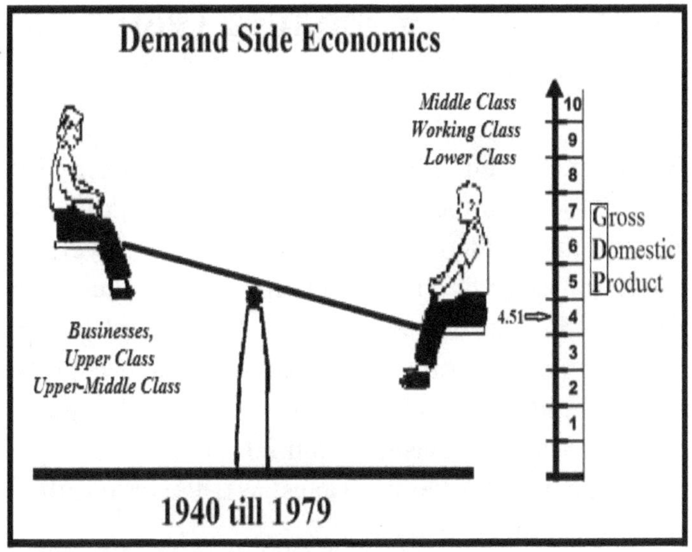

From 1940 to 1979 under Demand Side Economics, the U.S average yearly GDP was 4.51%.

Supply-Side Economics 1980's to the Present

President Reagan reduced income tax rates from 50% to 28% for the upper class and the upper-middle class, allowed tax deductions for business meals, travel, and entertainment,[58] and reduced corporate tax rates from 50% to 35%[59] as written into H.R.3838 - Tax Reform Act of 1986. As result of Reagan's 1981 and 1986 tax bills income tax rates for the upper class and upper-middle class were slashed from 70% to 28%[60] as CNN money reported in "Taxes: What people forget about Reagan.

In 1983, President Reagan allowed Social Security to be considered taxable income, thus, reducing individual Social Security benefits[61] according to the Social Security Administration's agency history, required Social Security Numbers to be able to claim and deduct dependents, raised the bottom income tax rate from 11% to 15%[62] for working class, and lower class, ended individual interest deductions for non-mortgage loans[63] and limited deductions for the middle class, the working class, and the lower class according to Investopedia's article "Tax Reform Act of 1986". Reagan required that itemized deductions be limited to amounts greater than 2% of adjusted gross income known as AGI and that medical expenses deductions be limited to amounts over 7.5% of AGI. Reagan repealed income tax deductions for State and local sales taxes negatively and disproportionately effecting middle class, working class and lower class. Reagan repealed the adoption expenses tax deduction which negatively affected the adoption of children by the middle and working classes. Under President Reagan's instructions, the Federal government appropriated, commandeered, and used the workers' Social Security Trust Reserve Funds to pay for government programs not related, connected, or associated with Social Security[64] according to FedSmith's article, "Ronal Reagan and the Great Social Security Heist." These actions by Reagan have had profound effects of lowering the demand for goods and services and lowering middle, working, and lower classes' annual wage growth from 2.4% to 1.8%. Under Reaganomics, the upper and upper-middle classes annual income growth more than doubled from 2.2% to 4.83%[65] according to Wikipedia's article "Reaganomics."

President Reagan, a former actor and sports broadcaster, used his communication skills to effectively manipulate, control, and deceive the middle, working and lower classes of taxpayers. He mastered placing one group against another, *"Divide and Conquer."* The groups that he pitted and compelled to fight, to compete against, and to despise each other included:

- Non-Union Workers versus Union Workers,
- Taxpayers versus welfare recipients,
- Whites versus people of color,
- Non-immigrants versus Immigrants,
- Old versus Young,

- Women versus Men,
- Christians versus Non-Christians,
- Pro-Life versus Pro-Choice,
- Straights versus LGBT (Lesbians, Gays, Bisexuals, and Transgenders),
- Conservatives versus Liberals,
- Middle Class versus Working Class,
- Etc.

Supply Side Economics commonly known as "Trickle-Down Economics" is the theory that by reducing the taxes paid by the companies, upper class, and upper-middle class, they would invest in the U.S. economy and these investments trickle down to the average taxpayers creating more opportunities, increase wages, and a better life.

The history of "Trickle-Down Economics" begins with the 1979 Republican Presidential Primary debates between Ronald Reagan and George H.W. Bush. George H.W. Bush stated that *"Supply Side Economics is Voodoo Economics."* Watch this 26-second video[66] titled "Bush Padre about Voodoo Economics." To receive campaign contributions from businesses, the upper class and upper-middle class, George H.W. Bush recanted this Voodoo Economics description of Supply Side Economics at their urging. This one correct and honest statement by George H.W. Bush *"Supply Side Economics is Voodoo Economics"* is the reason that he was not the Republican Presidential Candidate for 1980 and, therefore, did not become the Fortieth President.

Excuse the reference to "Trickle-Down Economics" as "Piss-on Economics," but, it clearly describes the effect on workers who create wealth through their labors.

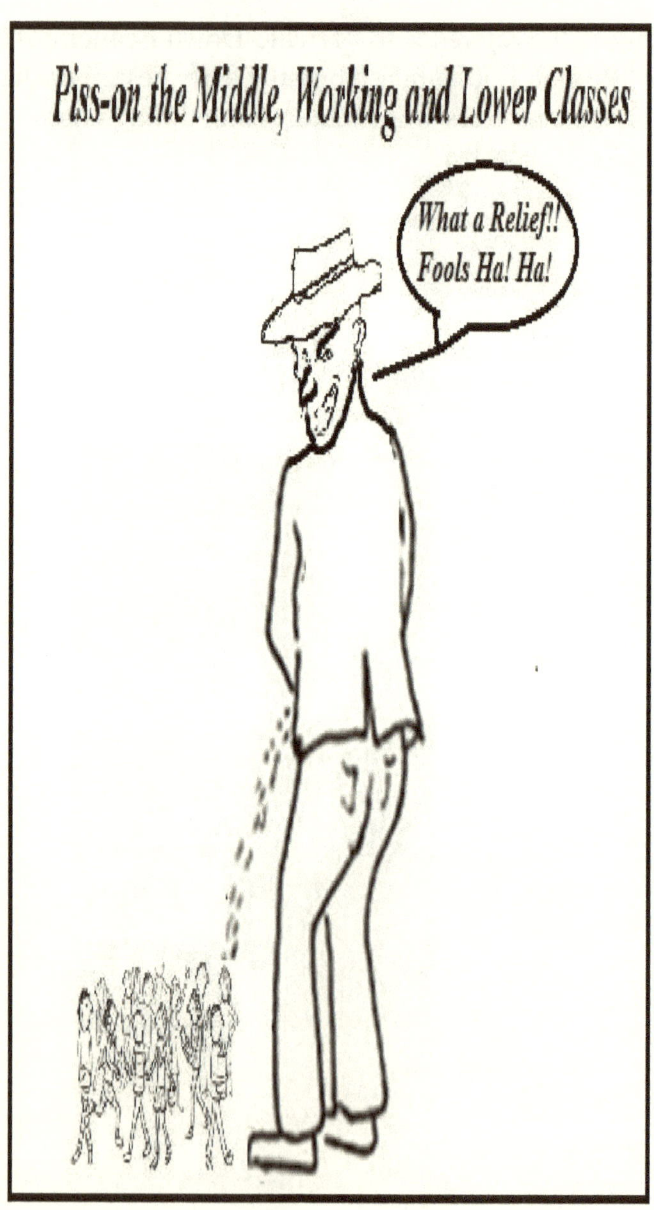
Piss-on the Middle, Working and Lower Classes
What a Relief!!
Fools Ha! Ha!
Piss-on the Middle, Working and Lower Classes

We do not need to beat it with a stick. But we need to actively help those politicians who believe in a "Balance Economy" get elected or re-elected.

One of the chief arguments for "Trickle Down Economics" or "Supply Side Economics" is that by allowing the job creators to have more money through fewer taxes, these job creators will invest in more factories and business creating more jobs.

Businesses will only create new factories, services, products and hire more employees if and only if, there is enough demand for their new services and products.

Demand for products and services comes not from the businesses but from the consumers.

Reversing the logic, demand for new products and services by consumers creates the need for new factories, services, and products. These new factories, services, and products generate the need for more employees. Therefore, the consumers, are the actual job creators via their increase in demand for products and services. Businesses are the demand opportunists in their pursuits and quests to increase their wealth.

If Businesses are given all the money in the world and if there is not a sufficient demand for these products or services to ensure a profit, businesses will never invest in new factories or other businesses.

If there is adequate demand for new products and services, businesses will always find the necessary money to invest and to exploit the consumer created, increased, and enlarged demands, markets, and needs for additional products and services.

Therefore, the true job creators are not businesses but are the consumers through their demand for more products and services.

The International Monetary Fund (IMF) in an article titled "Causes and Consequences of Income Inequality: A Global Perspective" has determined that "trickle-down" economics increases the wealth of Businesses, the upper class, and the upper-middle classes. Trickle-Down economics reduces the wealth of the middle, working and lower classes. This

Supply Side economics reduced GDP growth rather than increasing GDP growth[67] according to the IMF. From 1940 to 1979 under Demand Side Economics, the U.S. average yearly GDP was 4.51%. From 1980 to the present, the era of "Trickle-Down" economics, the U.S. average yearly GDP is just 2.64%. The Supply Side economics' GDP growth is almost 2% points lower than Demand-Side Economics. The affect, influence, and consequence of Trickle-Down Economics are reductions in the living standards and wealth for businesses, upper class, upper-middle, working class and lower class. From 1950 to 1979, the median house income increased from $24,000 to $34,000 and an increase of $10,000 represents an increase of 42% in buying power. From 1980 to present, the median house income increased from $48,462 to $53,657 and an increase of $5,195 or an increase of just 10% in buying power. This increase in wages is 4 times less under Supply Side Economics than Demand Side Economics. With a multiplier effect of 5 on the economy, this is a reduction in potential GDP growth of almost 20 times.

70% of the U.S. economy is the result of consumers purchases of products and services. This implies that reductions, limits, and cutbacks of additional, discretionary, and available money to purchase products and services reduces, cripples, and lames the growth of the economy, GDP. The limiting, reducing, and constraining of consumers' purchasing power of products and services began in 1980's under the Ronald Reagan administration. Ronald Reagan attacked unions stating falsely that they were responsible for the increases in the price of goods and services.

No business has ever determined the price of their products or services based upon the cost of those products or services and the additional amount for profits. Businesses sell their products and services based upon the market price.

What is the market price?

It is the amount of money that consumers are willing to pay for products and services regardless of the cost of producing products or providing services.

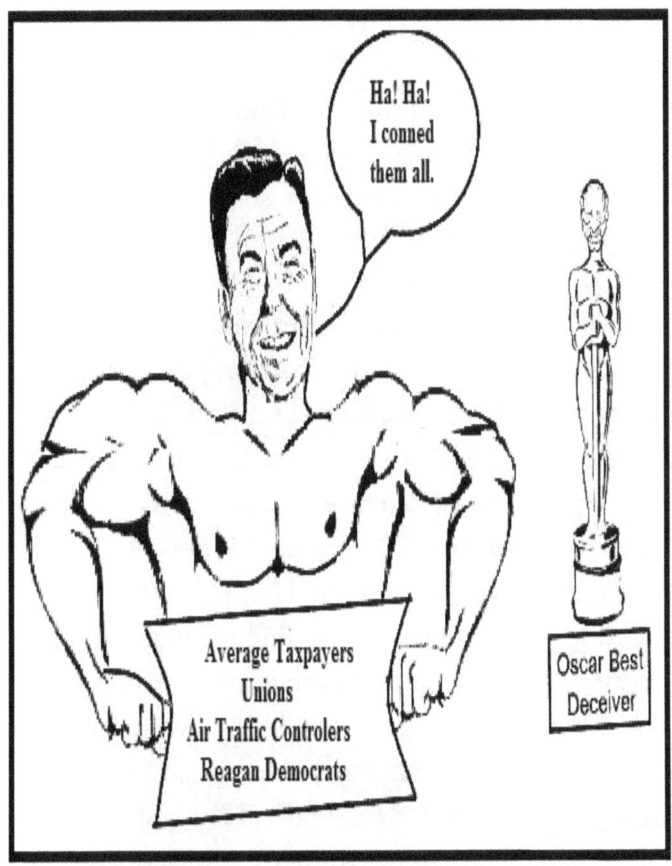

Unions were responsible for increasing the middle class from 1940 through 1980. Ronald Reagan by attacking unions reduced the middle class, reduced increases in the GDP to just 2.64% and reduced the wealth of businesses, upper class, and upper-middle class.

Balance Economics

Article 1 Section 8 of the U.S. Constitution states, "The Congress shall have Power To lay and collect Taxes, Duties, Imposts and Excises, to pay the Debts and provide for the common Defense and general Welfare of the United States." The U.S. Federal Government's primary constitutional duty is to defend the U.S. citizens and their properties from threats, foreign or domestic. The FY 2021 U.S. Defense budget is $740.5 billion according to the U.S. Department of Defense, release titled "DOD Releases Fiscal Year 2021 Budget Proposal".[68] This represents more than ½ of the U.S. Discretionary Spending. Discretionary Spending excludes Social Security, Medicare and Unemployment which are funded by Social Security Taxes, Medicare Taxes and Federal Unemployment taxes as reported by The Balance article titled "U.S. Federal Budget Breakdown."[69] These programs are viewed with distain, loathing and disgust by being described as entitlement giveaways not earned, deserved, or merited. These programs are not U.S. Federal government giveaways to the undeserving. Rather, workers have paid for these retirement, healthcare and unemployment programs through taxpayers' payroll and unemployment taxes. Rather than think of these programs as entitlements, one should understand these programs are taxpayer funded retirement, healthcare, and unemployment insurance programs. These insurance programs are to be there when needed, just like home property insurance or car insurance. No one would ever refer, call, or imply that homeowner's insurance is homeowners' entitlements.

Taxing at the same rate for all and taxing based on the effective footprint of each taxpayer is fair and balanced. A footprint is the number of products, goods, and services purchased or property owned by *taxpayers*, U.S. citizens or other identities paying taxes such as businesses, organizations, etc. The more that a *taxpayer* consumes, purchases, or owns, the higher is their effective footprint requiring greater, better, and larger U.S. defense protection. Balance economics is where *taxpayers* pay the same rate or percentage regardless of their effective footprint.

Balance Economics is balancing equally the burden and the cost of the U.S government's protection and defense of *taxpayers* and *taxpayers'* properties to the taxpayers' effective footprints based on consumption and assets. A *taxpayer* buys products, goods, and services. The number of products, goods, and services purchased is just one part of the *taxpayer's* effective protection and defense footprint. The more than a *taxpayer* consumes or purchases, the higher is the requirements for U.S. protection and defense. Businesses, the upper class, and the upper-middle class consume or purchase over 10,000 times more than the middle, working, and the lower classes consume or purchase. Thus, Business, upper class, and upper-middle class effective footprints requires 10,000 times more U.S. governmental resources to protect and to defend then for the middle, working, and the lower classes.

The U.S. government is a financial burden to, businesses, upper class, upper-middle class, middle class, working class, and lower class which ultimately hinders economic activity and growth for businesses and consumers alike. A Progressive Tax System increases the effective rate of taxes paid as the income increases. Our current income tax system is progressive in name and theory only. U.S. tax system is regressive in actual practice. A Regressive Tax System increases the effective tax rate for middle, working, and lower classes and decreases the effective tax rate for businesses, upper class, and upper-middle class.

It is unfair, discriminatory, and prejudicial to have income tax laws which allow businesses to deduct their business costs and not to allow employees their costs to earn wages, income.

- Businesses can deduct 100% of medical cost. Employees can deduct medical expenses that exceed 7.5% of their adjusted gross income.
- Businesses can deduct water expenses. Employees cannot.
- Businesses can deduct electric expenses. Employees cannot.

- Businesses can deduct gas expenses. Employees cannot.
- Businesses can deduct trash expenses. Employees cannot.
- Businesses can deduct training and educational expenses. Employees cannot deduct their training and education expenses.
- Businesses can deduct entertainment expenses. Employees cannot deduct Super Bowl Party expenses, etc.
- Businesses can deduct the cost of exercise equipment. Employees cannot deduct the cost of treadmills, stationary bikes, weights, weight machines, physical fitness memberships, etc.
- Businesses can deduct vehicle expenses. Employees cannot deduct transportation expenses.
- Businesses can deduct internet expenses. Employees cannot.
- Businesses can deduct telephone expenses. Employees cannot.
- Businesses can deduct cable TV expenses. Employees cannot.
- Businesses can deduct computer expenses. Employees cannot.
- Businesses can deduct 100% of interest on loans. Employees cannot deduct interest for car, personal, and educational loans.
- Businesses can deduct wellness programs. Employees cannot.

- Businesses can deduct postage. Employees cannot.
- Businesses can deduct meals. Employees cannot.
- Businesses can deduct rent. Employees cannot.
- Businesses can deduct laundry expenses. Employees cannot.
- Businesses can deduct cleaning supplies. Employees cannot.
- Businesses can deduct maintenance and repair cost. Employees cannot.
- Businesses can deduct clothing expenses. Employees cannot.
- Businesses can deduct child day care. Employees cannot.
- This is not an exhaustive list of what businesses can deduct that employees cannot.

It is surprising that the American Civil Liberties Union, ACLU, or anyone else have not challenged in court the unfair, inequitable, and discriminatory income tax laws.

In 2021, The Washington Post reported that 55 of the nation's largest corporations paid no federal income tax on more than $40 billion in profits. The Washing Post wrote that since the 2017 Trump tax cuts, 26 corporations have paid no federal income taxes on profits of more than $77 billion in profits while receiving nearly $5 billion in federal tax subsidies.[70] These 26 corporations had an effective tax rate of *not zero but a negative 6 percent* whereas a family earning $100,000 has an effective tax rate of 9.2%. This is just one example of how the progressive tax system in theory deforms, regresses, and evolves into a regressive tax system in practice.

Federal Income Taxes

26 Corporations Paid Zero Federal Income Tax

Average TaxPayer

Profits $77 Billion
Tax Credits $5 Billion
Tax Rate -6%

Income $100,000
Income Tax $9,200
Tax Rate 9.2%

ITEP, Institute on Taxation and Economy reported for fiscal year 2020 that at least 55 corporations paid zero federal income tax on $40.5 billion in U.S. pretax income for 2020 while receiving $3.5 billion in tax rebates or credits and avoiding $8.5 billion in taxes.[71] Their effective tax rate is -8.6% which states that these corporations are receiving government tax credits and rebates rather than paying taxes.

These tax credits or rebates are very similar to earn income credit which financially helps low-income workers and their families. In 2017 tax year, the average Earned Income Tax Credit (EITC) was $3,191 according to Center on Budget and Policy Priorities.[72] Many would call this well-fare or entitlements. By this logic, corporation tax rebates are a form of corporation welfare or entitlements.

Do profitable corporations deserve welfare checks?

The businesses, upper class, and upper-middle class pay a *lower effective tax rate* based on their income than the middle, working and lower classes. Since 1913, income taxes have become a permanent part of the U.S. life. Over the last 100 years, special interest groups have paid billions of dollars to politicians to change the income tax laws from being progressive to being regressive. These lobbyists' payoffs to politicians include campaign contributions, political ads, free lodgings, free travels, insider stock tips, and plenty of cash. The tax code is more than 73,954 pages with over 10 million words. The tax code manuals when stacked on top of each other are nearly 42 feet tall sourced from Walters Kluwer's Federal Tax Law Keeps Piling Up.

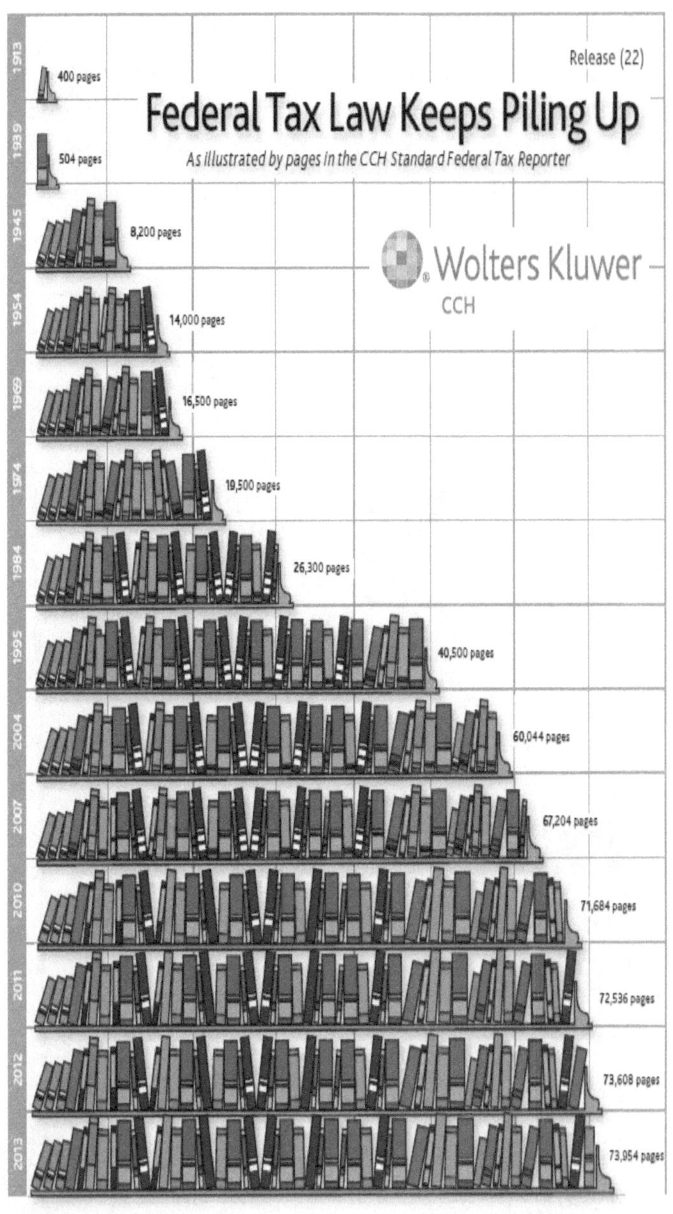
1913
400 pages
Release (22)
Federal Tax Law Keeps Piling Up
As illustrated by pages in the CCH Standard Federal Tax Reporter
Wolters Kluwer
CCH
1939
504 pages
1945
8,200 pages
1954
14,000 pages
1969
16,500 pages
1974
19,500 pages
1984
26,300 pages
1995
40,500 pages
2004
60,044 pages
2007
67,204 pages
2010
71,684 pages
2011
72,536 pages
2012
73,608 pages
2013
73,954 pages
Source: Wolters Kluwer, CCH: 2013
Permission for use granted.

From 1969 to 2013, there was a sudden, substantial, and directed increase of 54,454 pages in tax codes or an increase of 279%. These additional 54,454 pages of tax rules, regulations, and codes were tax breaks and loopholes that did not benefit the middle, working, or lower classes.

Senator Jeanne Shaeen Tweets *Warren Buffet, worth $44 Billion, Pays effectitve tax rate of 11%. Average tax rate is 13.5%. He's paying lower rate than his own secretary.*

Michael Bloomberg

Income taxes do not have any relationships to the constitutional duties and responsibilities of the federal government under the U.S. Constitution. The U.S. government has no constitutional obligation, duty, or responsibility to protect the income of taxpayers. Taxpayers can become bankrupted, lose revenue, or gain profits without Federal Government involvement, interest, or engagement.

"The federal government has the sole constitutional duty and responsibility to protect the U.S. citizens and their properties from harm, theft, and war."

Our founding fathers placed in the Preamble to the U.S. Constitution that the federal government is responsible for national defense.

The Preamble to the U.S. Constitution states:

"We the people of the United States, in order to form a more perfect union, establish justice, ensure domestic tranquility, provide for the common defense, promote the general welfare, and secure the blessings of liberty to ourselves and our posterity, do ordain and

establish this Constitution for the United States of America."

A simple, easy, and unembellished tax system that reflects the cost of U.S. government's constitutional duty to protect the citizens and their properties is needed, required and long overdue. This simple and easy tax filling would require just a 1-page form and 1 hour to complete and file for the most taxpayers.

A 1.5% federal sale tax and 1.5% federal property tax would pay for the U.S. government's constitutional duty to protect taxpayers and their properties.

The U.S. military ensures that relatively safe global trade occurs throughout the world's oceans, throughout the world's sky's and throughout the world's lands. The U.S subsidizes the defense of other nations by paying 36% of the world's defense spending; this is equivalent to what the top eight countries behind the U.S. spend on their militaries combined. A U.S. defense import duty, a value-added tax of 10%, is warranted and would fund the U.S. defense of world trade.

Eliminating all other forms of taxes except for Social Security, Medicare and Federal Unemployment taxes and replacing them with a 1.5% federal sales tax, a 1.5% federal property tax and a 10% Defense Value Added Import tax would fully fund the government and in time pay off the national debt.

It is debatable, controversial, and questionable as to the constitutionality of federal sales and property taxes. Rather than enter an academic discussions, debates, and conversations as to the constitutionality of the federal sales and property taxes, the U.S. should merely, simply, and easily pass a new constitutional amendment. The 16th Amendment, the income tax amendment, required 4 years or 2 national elections to be ratified.

A 28th Constitutional Amendment allowing the federal government to collect sales and property tax would be a fair and balanced taxation system that would be the same tax rate for every taxpayer. The 28th Amendment, Sales and Property Taxes, would allow the government of the U.S. to accomplish, achieve and pay for the U.S. constitutional requirement to protect the citizens and their properties. An act of congress, the Fair and Balanced Sales, Property, and Defense Import Taxes Act, (FABSPDITA), would nullify, abolish, and end other forms of U.S. federal taxes such as income, estate (death tax), inheritance, gift, hotel, excise tax, highway usage, gambling, airport, tobacco, alcohol, etc. taxes.

Sales and Property Taxes and FABSPDITA

- Taxes would be easier, more straightforward, and simpler to file, one hour for most taxpayers as opposed, compared, and judged against the average of 53 hours to file income taxes.
- Future Changes to FABSPDITA would require a 2/3 congressional majority to alter, change, or update. This would limit, reduce, and possibly eliminate the bribing of politicians to corrupt FABSPDITA as happened with the current U.S. income tax laws.
- FABSPDITA would maintain a consistent, predictable, and congruous tax revenue from year to year allowing for reliable, predictable, and practical U.S. multi-year budget planning. The revenue as provided by the current U.S. Income tax system varies from year to year and is depended on the taxpayers' incomes and the health of the U.S. economy. Recessions, depressions, severe weather disasters, pandemics, etc. have caused and will cause the U.S. income tax revenue to decline, to fluctuate, and to be unpredictable. The Great Recession of 2008 reduced U.S. income tax revenue by

> almost 20%. The Great Depression of
> 1929 reduced U.S. income tax revenue by
> almost 25%.
>
> - FABSPDITA would immediately and
>   fully fund the government and in time pay
>   down U.S. national debt.

In this model, the tax burden would be shared equally for all taxpayers paying the same 1.5% rate for federal property taxes and sales taxes. It would neither be Demand or Supply Side Economics but Balanced Economics. FABSPDITA would significantly reduce the possibility of high inflation, a product of demand-side economics and severe recession, a typical characteristic of supply-side economics. As a result, a steady rise of the nation's GDP without extreme downturns and without high periods of inflation would occur. By balancing the burden of the U.S. Government equally, and by not favoring businesses, upper class and upper middle class, an immediate increase in the annual GDP from the meager 2.64% of Supply Side Economics would be seen. Eventually, the expected yearly GDP growth would be higher than 4.51% of the Demand Side Economics. How much higher than 4.51% GDP annual increase is difficult to determine. However, based on the 2% spread between Supply Side and Demand Side Economics, it is reasonable to expect an annual increase in GDP to be between 5.51% and 6.51%. The increase in GDP would increase, grow, and create more wealth for all, businesses, upper class, upper-middle class, middle class, working class and lower class.

The federal government would have a steady, constant, and predictable amount of revenue, year after year. Therefore, the government could better plan for future expenditures.

Metaphorically, as an example, both the U.S. economy and grass grow best when the nutrients required to grow them is equally distributed. For lawns, potassium is needed for roots to grow. Similarly, for the U.S. Economy demand is required for the economy to expand. Nitrogen is necessary for healthy green lawns, just as revenue is needed to create new businesses. The two work in tandem. So as an increase in demand occurs an increase in revenue follows. Balancing the burden of the United

States government equally among all taxpayers creates more wealth and money for everyone.

From 1980-2016, Supply Side Economics with an average GDP rate of 2.6% increased GDP to $16 trillion.

Under Demand Side Economics with an average GDP rate of 4.5% from 1980-2016, the GDP would have grown to $32 trillion.

Under Balance Economics with an average GDP rate of 6.5% from 1980-2016, GDP would have grown to $62 trillion. A balanced economic approach would increase GDP by almost four times greater than that of Supply Side Economics. This has the effect of increasing the wealth for all.

Truly, Rising Tides Lift All Boats. As previously asserted by New England Chamber of Commerce and later attributed to President John F. Kennedy, *"A rising tide lifts all boats."*

As increases and improvements in the GDP happen, the overall economy would end up working in favor of all participants. Hopefully, all taxpayers will understand that Balance Economics increases their wealth by a product of 4, 4 times greater.

Realizing 28th Amendment and FABSPDITA

This 28th Amendment requires two thirds of both the House of Representatives and the Senate of U.S. to vote for passage of the amendment and 3/4th of the state legislatures to ratify the 28th Amendment. It appears difficult, if not impossible, to accomplish. Despite this, there is a simple, easy, and straight forward strategy to making the 28th Amendment a reality. The 16th Amendment Income tax was introduced in 1909 and ratified in 1913. The 28th Amendment may need several election cycles to elect state and federal legislators that support and will vote for the 28th Amendment and to remove from office state and federal legislators that do not support and would vote against the 28th Amendment.

Taxpayers and *Voters Like You* will need:

- To elect a president who supports the *28th Amendment and FABSPDITA*,
- To elect a president who will create a whitehouse.gov page that identifies Senators, House Representatives and state legislators who support the *28th Amendment and FABSPDITA*,
- To vote for and to elect Senators and Congressman/woman and legislators at the state level that endorse, support, and agree with the *28th Amendment and FABSPDITA*

and will ratify the 28th Amendment and vote for FABSPDITA.

Politicians, in the pocket of special interest groups, will defy the wishes, needs, and wants of *Voters Like You* and not vote to pass, ratify, and enact the *28th Amendment and FABSPDITA*. *Voters Like You* will vote these defiant, insubordinate, and arrogant politicians out of office. *Voters Like You* need to be patient allowing for multiple election cycles to eliminate politicians who are not representing the voting majority's wills, desires, and aspirations. The bottom line is that politicians serve at the pleasure of *Voters Like You*. You have the great power of voting them into or out of political offices. Use your authority, strength, and power to fire those who would defy your desire to have a fair and balanced tax system.

The 28th Amendment reads:

The Congress shall have power to lay and collect taxes on property and sales from whatever source derived, without apportionment among the states, and without regard to any census or enumeration.

False 28th and FABSPDITA Arguments

Those on a fixed income would not be able to afford the 1.5% property tax and their homes could be taken. Therefore, those on fixed incomes may lose their homes and may become homeless.

A provision of *FABSPDITA* would allow the low fixed income elderly to remain in their homes. When the home is sold or inherited, the accumulated property tax would be due and paid.

FABSPDITA would stifle business growth and hurt the economy.

This is untrue because taxpayers would have increased disposable income, which would lead to a greater demand for goods and services, and result in more employees hired to meet this increasing demand. Those perpetuating and propagating this falsehood, myth, and deception do not want to pay the same fair and balanced tax rate as all other taxpayers pay.

For an example, a wealthy individual having $100 billion in property and a typical median taxpayer household having $100 thousand in property would both pay the same property tax of 1.5%. Thus, the wealthy individual would pay $1.5 billion in taxes whereas the typical taxpayer would pay $1,500. This is fair and balanced since the taxes correlate, correspondent, and relate to the cost of the military protection for $100 billion in property. This is 1,000,000 times higher, greater, and costlier than the resources, equipment, and soldiers required, apportioned, and needed to protect $100 thousand in property. Typically, the upper class, like Warren

Buffet, with $100 billion in property, capital, and wealth pays about $1.8 million in federal income tax. Whereas the typical taxpayer with $100 thousand in property who earns about $56 thousand per year in income and pays $7,000 in federal income tax.

If the typical taxpayer spends 90% of their earned income, or $50 thousand, the federal sales tax would be $750. The federal property tax would be $1,500, 1.5% of $100,000 worth of property. For the typical taxpayer, the total for federal sales tax and the federal property tax is $2,250. This is about $5,000 less than they pay under the current income taxes. This additional disposable income buys more goods and services. The typical taxpayer would spend about 80% of the $5,000 or $4,000, saving the rest. Multiplying $4,000 by 126 million households equates to $.5 trillion added to U.S. GDP. This is a lot of unrealized pent-up, repressed, and unexpressed demand for goods and services. Given the U.S. GDP is about $16 trillion, this $.5 trillion would represent an additional growth of 3.1% in GDP. U.S. GDP growth per year would rise from 2.6% to 5.7%.

This does not include the "Multiplier Effect." The "Multiplier Effect" assumes that a household has an additional $5 thousand to spend. This household will pay out 80% of $5 thousand on various goods and services. The vendors and business will receive an additional $4 thousand in revenue and spend 80% or $3,200 on wages, floor space, machines, and equipment. This cycle of 80% spending of additional income or revenue continues producing a multiplier effect of 5 times. The typical taxpayer's increase in spending of $4,000 would increase economic activity of $20 thousand.

With the multiplier effect of 5, $.5 trillion in tax savings for the typical taxpayer would expand, swell, and increase economic growth, GDP by $2.5 trillion. This $2.5 trillion would be an increase in GDP of 16%. This GDP growth is incredible, fantastic, and sounds too good to be true. The numbers do not lie. This increase in economic activity is predictable, possible, and probable.

Given that the average upper class would pay over 800 times more than what they currently pay, $1.8 million as compared to $1.5 billion for $100 billion worth of property. The wealthy taxpayer will fight with every tool available legal, illegal, and immoral in order not to pay the same tax rate of 1.5% as all other taxpayers pay. The upper class will use the media, internet, fake news, newspapers, magazines, politicians, economist, intimidation, etc. The upper class want others to bear the cost of protecting their wealth, property, and capital. The upper class will attempt to delay, hinder, and obstruct the passage, enactment, and ratification of the 28th Amendment and FABSPDITA. But the upper class will not be able to permanently block, obstruct and stop *Voters Like You* from electing politicians that support and will vote for the 28th Amendment and FABSPDITA.

Misleading arguments against FABSPDITA

FABSPDITA would be difficult and costly to enforce and implement.

The current income tax code is over 16 thousand pages of regulations, and it is being enforced and implement. The *FABSPDITA* would require less than 30 pages of regulations. By reducing the complicated nature of taxes, the U.S. government would save an immense amount of time and money which could be utilized in different ways to serve all taxpayers. The typical taxpayer would require one single paged tax form and just an hour to prepare, complete, and file.

The 28th FABSPDITA would hurt charities, religions, and other nonprofits by taxing their property and by not giving tax breaks for donations.

The donors will still receive a tax break by no longer owning the donated property. Therefore, the donors would not pay this 1.5% property on that property which has been donated. The 1.5% property tax on nonprofit's assets is the same as for everyone else. Is this not fair?

Why should the U.S. government determine who should be a non-profit entity not paying taxes and who should be a for-profit entity paying taxes? *Both bask in safety under the defense and protection of the U.S. government.*

The 10% defense import tax would increase prices causing all to pay more for imported goods.

This is based on the false premise that businesses determine the selling price of item by the cost to manufacture the products and their profit margins, Cost-Plus Profit. Price for goods and services are determined by the Market Price and not by the Cost-Plus Profit price. The market price or selling price is determined by, whatever, consumers are willing to pay for products.

An excellent example of Market Price is the cost of a golf club driver. Every golfer knows that longer drives from the teeing area will shorten the course resulting in a better and lower score, strokes per round. Therefore, golfers are willing to pay high prices for gaining greater distance from the tee. Drivers that promise this increase in distance will cost the consumer between $200 to $400 each. The cost to manufacture these same drivers is less than $60 per driver. If golfers were only willing to pay $100 for a driver than retailers would sell their drivers for $100. *"If a good golf game could be bought, there would be many good golf games".*

With the 10% Defense Import Tax, the golf club manufacturers would continue to sell their drivers for $200 to $400 since that is the market price. These golf club manufacturers would see a small loss in their profit of $20 to $40 per driver sold. The profit would now be $120 to $300 per driver sold.

Therefore, the 10% Defense Import Tax would not affect the retail price of goods but result in a slight reduction in profit for overseas manufacturers and import brokers.

This does include the fact that based on the 10% Defense Import tax that many companies would move their manufacturing of products back to the U.S. The current cost index between China and the U.S.A is just 5%, 95 to 100. See Manufacturing Cost index, extracted from the internet article, "U.S. Manufacturing costs are almost as low as China's, and that's a huge deal" July 26, 2015.[73]

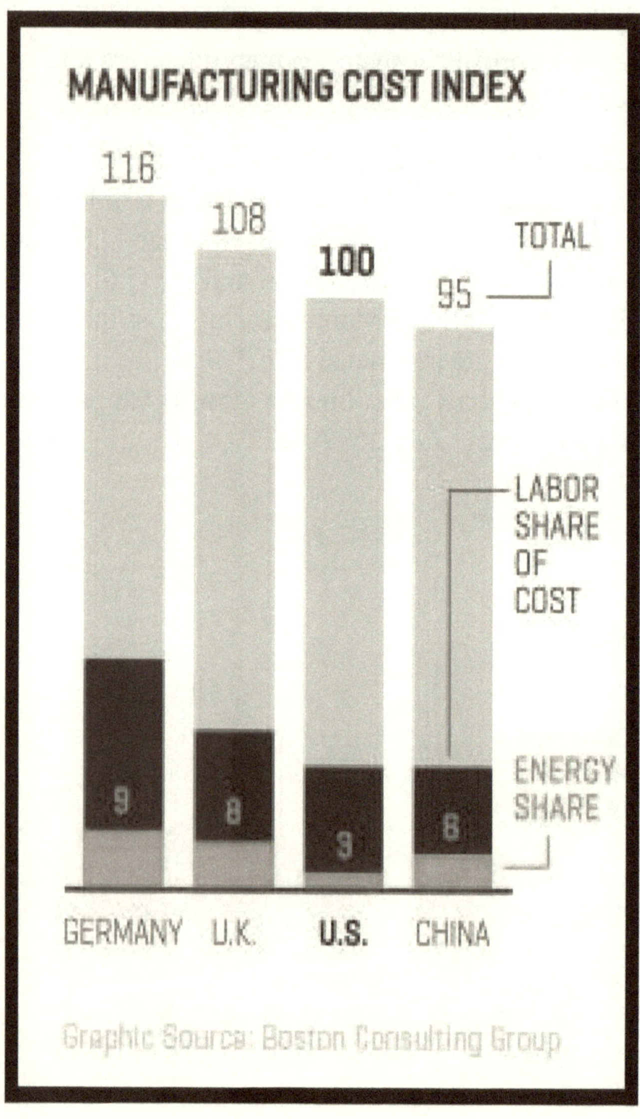

Since the cost of manufacturing in China is just 5%
less than the manufacturing cost in the U.S., many

Pg. 124

international companies will locate or more accurately relocate their factories back to the U.S. This relocation back to the U.S. will create more jobs in the U.S., will increase the demand for goods and services and will raise the U.S.'s GDP. The trade imbalance with China is $200 billion per year. If just half of this trade imbalance with China, an additional $100 billion would be manufactured in the U.S. The multiplier effect, a factor of 5 would cause this $100 billion to increase the U.S.'s GDP by $500 billion or an increase in GDP by almost 3%.

The taxpayers currently pay for the U.S. military's defense of global trade routes by ocean, by air and by land. A 10% defense import tax simply acknowledges this fact by assessing a tax on products imported to U.S

Because of "Market Price," the consumer will pay very little if any increase for imported goods. Because of the "Relocation of Manufacturing Back to the U.S.," the consumer would benefit from increased employment opportunities.

I hate filling taxes. It is frustrating.

It's too long. It waste my time.

Annually, taxpayers waste 8.1 billion hours to comply with tax code filings at an estimated cost of $200 billion. $30 billion is spent annually on tax filing software, tax preparation fees, etc. The hours wasted by individuals throughout the year include collecting, sorting, and filing receipts and payments, accounting of receipts and payments via electronic or manual spreadsheets, filling out taxes manually or using tax software and mailing or electronic transfer of the tax forms. An average taxpayer spends or simply waste 53 hours per year to meet the obligation to pay and to file taxes according to American Action Forum report titled "Tax Day 2018: Compliance Costs Approach $200 billion" by Dan Bosch and Gordon Gray.[74]

Making Taxing Fair and Balance a Reality

Voters Like You need:
- To vote for a president who supports Taxing Fair and Balance, FABSPDITA, and the 28th Constitutional Amendment.
- To choose a president who creates a whitehouse.gov page that identifies Senators and House Representatives who support:
  - Taxing Fair and Balance,
  - FABSPDITA, and
  - the 28th Constitutional Amendment.
- To vote for and to elect Senators and Representatives at both the federal and state level that support:

- o   Taxing Fair and Balance,
- o   FABSPDITA, and
- o   the 28th Constitutional Amendment.

Applying Political Pressure for better and less expensive healthcare will be accomplished by:

- Voting,
- Telephoning your Congressional Representatives and your Senators,
- Writing to your Congressional Representatives and your Senators,
- Emailing your Congressional Representatives and your Senators,
- Visiting your Congressional Representatives' and your Senator's offices in your state,
- Visiting your Congressional Representatives' and your Senator's offices in Washington DC,
- Attending your Congressional Representatives' and your Senator's locally held town halls,
- Lobbying of your Congressional Representatives and your Senators,
- Marching and demonstrating,
- Calling political talk radio stations,
- Donating to Congressional Representatives and Senators who support Taxing Fair and Balance, and
- Volunteering in Congressional Representatives' and Senators' campaigns.

Through the actions above by *Voters Like You*, *Taxing Fair and Balance* will become a reality.

References

[1] https://en.wikipedia.org/wiki/List_of_U.S._presidential_campaign_slogans

[2] https://www.militaryfactory.com/vietnam/casualties.asp

[3] https://www.thebalance.com/u-s-inflation-rate-history-by-year-and-forecast-3306093

[4] https://millercenter.org/president/ronald-reagan/key-events

[5] https://millercenter.org/president/ronald-reagan/key-events

[6] https://www.politico.com/story/2018/12/24/bush-pardons-iran-contra-felons-dec-24-1992-1072042

[7] https://millercenter.org/president/george-h-w-bush/key-events

[8] https://smartasset.com/mortgage/the-pros-and-cons-of-nafta

[9] https://millercenter.org/president/bill-clinton/key-events

[10] https://millercenter.org/president/george-w-bush/key-events

[11] https://millercenter.org/president/george-w-bush/key-events

[12] https://millercenter.org/president/trump/key-events

[13] https://www.politifact.com/factchecks/2017/sep/20/bernie-s/comparing-administrative-costs-private-insurance-a/"

[14] https://www.verywellhealth.com/health-insurance-companies-unreasonable-profits-1738941

[15] https://revcycleintelligence.com/news/insurance-and-medical-billing-costs-for-providers-reaches-282bt

[16] https://www.cms.gov/Research-Statistics-Data-and-Systems/Statistics-Trends-and-Reports/NationalHealthExpendData/NHE-Fact-Sheet

[17] https://www.policygenius.com/health-insurance/out-of-pocket-expenses/

[18] http://www.nbcnews.com/storyline/va-hospital-scandal/va-numbers-how-big-it-who-uses-it-n101771

[19] http://www.blogs.va.gov/VAntage/13790/va-rates-high-on-patient-satisfaction-in-national-survey/

[20] https://www.cnbc.com/2018/02/22/medical-errors-third-leading-cause-of-death-in-america.html

[21] https://www.imprivata.com/patient-misidentification

[22] https://www.imprivata.com/patient-misidentification

[23] https://www.ncbi.nlm.nih.gov/pmc/articles/PMC4512870/

[24] https://www.myhealth.va.gov/

25 https://www.ncbi.nlm.nih.gov/pmc/articles/PMC4908687/

26 https://www.ncbi.nlm.nih.gov/pubmed/23027317/

27 https://www.ncbi.nlm.nih.gov/pmc/articles/PMC4106580/

28 https://www.va.gov/health/aboutvha.asp

29 https://www.everycrsreport.com/reports/RL33802.html

30 https://www.research.va.gov/MVP/default.cfm

31 https://www.va.gov/opa/pressrel/pressrelease.cfm?id=5125

32 https://www.blogs.va.gov/VAntage/tag/nobel-prize/

33 https://www.va.gov/opa/pressrel/pressrelease.cfm?id=5113

34 https://www.healthsystemtracker.org/chart-collection/u-s-spending-healthcare-changed-time/#item-nhe-trends_total-national-health-expenditures-us-trillions-1987-2018

35 https://fas.org/sgp/crs/misc/RS22897.pdf

36 https://www.verywellhealth.com/why-do-i-wait-so-long-at-the-doctors-office-2615092

37 https://www.aafp.org/fpm/2003/0600/p27.html

38 https://www.pharmacychecker.com/askpc/how-can-i-determine-where-a-drug-is-manufactured/#!

39 https://www.scientificamerican.com/article/how-the-u-s-pays-3-times-more-for-drugs/?redirect=1

40 https://www.ncbi.nlm.nih.gov/books/NBK50972/

41 https://www.cdc.gov/pcd/issues/2019/18_0625.htm

42 https://www.cdc.gov/publichealthgateway/didyouknow/topic/phs.html

43 https://www.healthcare.gov/preventive-care-adults/

44 https://newsatjama.jama.com/2017/09/27/jama-forum-the-high-costs-of-unnecessary-care/

45 http://www.commonwealthfund.org/publications/issue-briefs/2015/oct/us-health-care-from-a-global-perspective

46 https://www.health.ny.gov/regulations/hcra/univ_hlth_care.htm

47 https://www.healthsystemtracker.org/chart-collection/how-do-healthcare-prices-and-use-in-the-u-s-compare-to-other-countries/#item-the-u-s-has-consistently-had-much-shorter-average-hospital-stays-than-patients-in-comparable-countries_2018

48 http://www.americashealthrankings.org/learn/reports/2016-annual-report/comparison-with-other-nations

49 https://economix.blogs.nytimes.com/2009/07/15/how-much-do-doctors-in-other-countries-make/

50 https://www.nytimes.com/2016/11/08/upshot/a-doctor-shortage-lets-take-a-closer-look.html

51 https://www.cnbc.com/2015/04/30/doctor-shortages-heres-the-real-culprit-commentary.html

52 https://www.cnbc.com/2015/04/30/doctor-shortages-heres-the-real-culprit-commentary.html

53 https://www.webmd.com/a-to-z-guides/news/20020927/5-of-doctors-50-of-malpractice

54 http://www.npr.org/sections/health-shots/2016/05/03/476636183/death-certificates-undercount-toll-of-medical-errors

55 Henry Ford, the founder of Ford Motor Company

56 Henry Ford, the founder of Ford Motor Company

57 http://www.kff.org/health-costs/report/2016-employer-health-benefits-survey/

58 https://www.congress.gov/bill/99th-congress/house-bill/3838

59 https://www.investopedia.com/terms/t/taxreformact1986.asp
60

https://money.cnn.com/2010/09/08/news/economy/reagan_years_taxes/index.htm

61 https://www.ssa.gov/history/taxationofbenefits.html

62 https://www.investopedia.com/terms/t/taxreformact1986.asp

63 https://www.britannica.com/topic/Tax-Reform-Act

64 https://www.fedsmith.com/2013/10/11/ronald-reagan-and-the-great-social-security-heist/

65 https://en.wikipedia.org/wiki/Reaganomics

66 https://www.youtube.com/watch?v=X2UAuFArbOY

67 https://www.imf.org/en/Publications/Staff-Discussion-Notes/Issues/2016/12/31/Causes-and-Consequences-of-Income-Inequality-A-Global-Perspective-42986

68 https://www.defense.gov/Newsroom/Releases/Release/Article/2079489/dod-releases-fiscal-year-2021-budget-proposal/

69 https://www.thebalance.com/u-s-federal-budget-breakdown-3305789

70 https://www.washingtonpost.com/business/2021/04/05/corporations-federal-taxes/

71 https://itep.org/55-profitable-corporations-zero-corporate-tax/

72 https://www.cbpp.org/research/federal-tax/the-earned-income-tax-credit

73 http://fortune.com/2015/06/26/fracking-manufacturing-costs/

74 https://www.americanactionforum.org/research/tax-day-2018-compliance-costs-approach-200-billion/